Voyage of the Sable Venus and Other Poems

# Voyage of the Sable Venus

## AND OTHER POEMS

Robin Coste Lewis

ALFRED A. KNOPF   NEW YORK   2019

THIS IS A BORZOI BOOK
PUBLISHED BY ALFRED A. KNOPF

Grateful acknowledgment is made to the following for permission
to reprint previously published material:

BOA Editions Ltd.: "a dream of foxes" from *The Collected Poems of Lucille Clifton,* copyright
© 1996 by Lucille Clifton. Reprinted by permission of The Permissions Company, Inc. on
behalf of BOA Editions Ltd., www.boaeditions.org.

Jean Valentine and Alice James Books: Excerpt from *Lucy: A Poem,* copyright © 2009
by Jean Valentine. Reprinted with permission of The Permissions Company, Inc.,
on behalf of the author and Alice James Books, www.alicejamesbooks.org.

Page 162 constitutes an extension of the copyright page.

Library of Congress Cataloging-in-Publication Data
Lewis, Robin Coste.
[Poems. Selections]
Voyage of the Sable Venus and other poems / Robin Coste Lewis.—First edition.
pages  cm
"This is a Borzoi book."
ISBN 978-1-101-87543-8 (hardcover)—ISBN 978-1-101-87544-5 (ebook)—
ISBN 978-1-101-91120-4 (trade pbk.)
I. Title.
PS3612.E98A6 2016
811'.6—dc23
2014047762

Cover photograph: *Window Shopping* by Eudora Welty. Reprinted by permission of the
Mississippi Department of Archives and History and Russell & Volkening as agents for the
author. Copyright © by Eudora Welty, renewed by Eudora Welty, LLC.
Cover design by Stephanie Ross

Manufactured in the United States of America
Published September 29, 2015
First Paperback Edition, November 21, 2017
Second Printing, April 2019

*for*

BEAUTY

Lucy
your secret book
that you leaned over and wrote just in the dirt—
Not having to have an ending
Not having to last

—JEAN VALENTINE

# Contents

I

# Plantation

And then one morning we woke up
embracing on the bare floor of a large cage.

To keep you happy, I decorated the bars.
Because you had never been hungry, I knew

I could tell you the black side
of my family owned slaves.

I realize this is perhaps
the one reason why I love you,

because I told you this
and you—still—wanted to kiss

me. We laughed when I said *plantation,*
fell into our chairs when I said *cane.*

There were fingers on the floor
and the split bodies of women

who'd been torn apart by horses
during the Inquisition.

You'd said, *Well I'll be damned!*
Every now and then you'd change

from a prancing black buck
into a small high yellow girl: pigtailed,

patent leather, eyes spinning gossamer, begging
for egg salad and banana pudding.

Or just as quickly you'd become
the girl's mother, pulling

yourself away from yourself.
Because my whole head was covered

with a heaving beehive, you thought
I didn't notice. I noticed. I cried honey.

And then you were fourteen, and you had grown
a glorious steel cock under your skirt. To brag

you rubbed yourself against me. Then your tongue
was inside my mouth, and I wanted to say

*Please ask me first,* but it was your
tongue, so who cared suddenly

about your poor manners?
We had books and a waterfall

was falling in the corner.
I didn't tell you I couldn't

remember what that thing was
you said to me once, that tender thing

you'd said I should never forget.
The moment you said it, I forgot it.

I wondered if you thought we were lost.
We weren't lost. We were *loss.*

And meanwhile, all I could think about
were the innumerable ways I would've loved

to have eaten you, how being
devoured can make one cry. And I hoped

you liked the fresh, pleasant taste
of juiced cane. You pulled

my pubic bone toward you. I didn't
say, *It's still broken;* I didn't tell

you, *There's still this crack.* It was sore,
but I stayed silent because you were smiling.

You said, *The bars look pretty, Baby,*
then rubbed your hind legs up against me.

# On the Road to Sri Bhuvaneshwari

I.

Not much larger than a Volkswagen. Smiling
    on the dashboard: Gurumukh. Marigolds
        so mild we can chew. What we call *mountain*
            they say *foothill.* A whole vibrant green

valley of terraced balconies, rectangular
    rice farms carved into every façade
        for seven centuries. Now and then
            a clay road washed out by rain. We wait.

Barefoot men in madras dhotis, bodies
    large only as necessity, hoist twice that in boulders
        back up the mountain, back to that place
            where the road had been.

Monsoon. Uttar Pradesh. Twenty-eight days of rain.
    At dinner, someone says, During
        the nineteenth century, all this water
        caused the British to go

mad. They constantly committed suicide.
    Later, someone else
        points out their Victorian cemetery.
        I smile—a little.

That morning, seven langurs the size of six-
    year-olds, grey and brown, white and beige, tall tails
        curling, jumped up and down, shucked
            and jived on top of my cold tin roof.

Somehow, I am still alive.
     I know it is wrong
          to think of a decade as lost.
               The more I recover, the more I go

blind. Squat
     naked beside a steaming bucket.
          Hold a small cloth.
               In Trinidad, one says *clot.*

The *h* is quiet.
     A wafer of breath—just
          like here. There's no telling
               what languishes inside the body.

Not mist, but a whole cloud
     passes into one window,
          then two hours later,
               out the other.

My American college students try out
     their kindergarten Hindi: *ha-pee-tal,*
          *ha-pee-tal.* Lips finger the sign's script,
               then the United States break

open their mouths
     into sad smiles when they realize
          it's not Hindi, but English
               written in Devanagari: *hospital.*

For the whole day we drive
     along miles of wet, slithering clay
          to find a temple at the top of a *mountain*
               where Shiva is said to have once dropped

a piece of Parvati.
     Every mountaintop made holy
          by the falling charred body part
               of the Goddess. An elbow fell

here; here
            fell Her toe; an ankle—black
                    and burnt—Her knee. The road is wet and dark
                            red, and keeps spinning.

I sit behind the driver, admiring
            his cinnamon fingers, his coiffed white beard,
                    his pale pink turban wrapped so handsomely.
                            *Why did it take all that?*

*I mean, why did She have to jump*
            *into the celestial fire*
                    *to prove Her purity?*
                            *Shiva's cool—poisonous, blue,*

*a shimmering galaxy—*
            *but when it came to His Old Lady,*
                    *man, He fucked up!*
                            *Why couldn't He just believe Her?*

I joke with the driver. We laugh.
            Gurumukh smiles back. But then I think, perhaps
                    embodiment is so bewildering, even God grows
                            wrecked with doubt.

For a certain amount
            of rupees, the temple's hired a man
                    to announce to tourists . . . *During the medieval period*
                            *virgins were sacrificed here.*

His capitalist glance mirrors our Orientalist tans.
            *You're lying,* I say. *Save it*
                    *for somebody pale.* He smiles, passes
                            me a bidi. I'm bleeding, but lie

so I can go inside and see
            that burnt, charred piece
                    of the Goddess that fell off
                            right here.

We climb up another one hundred
        and eight stairs. At the top, I try
                not to listen to anyone.
                        An entire Himalayan valley. Chiseled.

Every mountain—peak to base—
        a terraced living verdant staircase
                for the Goddess to walk down:
                *Sri Bhuvaneshwari.*

II.

At night, our caravan winds back
        over gravel and clay. Ten headlamps
                grope the mountain walls
                        of the green-black valley. The road

is only as wide as one small car. Hours of dog
        elbows, switchbacks, half roads.
                Slowly after a turn, the driver takes his foot
                        off the gas, downshifts, coasts.

Black.    Warm.    Breath.    Snorting.
        Our car rubs against one biting grass off the face
                of a cliff. Then another, taller
                        than our car. Then hundreds

block the road. Thick cylindrical horns scrape
        the driver's window; eyes so white, black
                pupils gleam, peering into our cab, grunting
                        and drooling onto the window.

Now the whole car, surrounded. Warm black bodies
        covered in fur. Near their dusty hooves, children
                sit on the ground, nested in laps, quiet and smiling.
                        Everyone embroidered with color:

silvers, metallic ochres, kohls, golds, reds, bold
          blacks, all of it—and a green so green
                    I realize it's a shade
                    I have never seen.

A whole nomadic clan, traveling
          with hundreds of water buffalo. At least
                    sixty human beings. There are so many
                              buffalo, our cars cannot move. And they can't move

the herd because a few feet ahead
          a She-Buffalo is giving birth.
                    We get out.
                              And wait.

Out of habit, the students pull out their American sympathy,
          but then the driver says all the women sitting there
                    on the ground, dusty, with children in their laps, dangling
                              their ankles over the mountain, adorned—all—

wear enough gold, own enough
          buffalo to buy your whole house—cash.
                    The night holds. Life is giving birth
                              in the middle of a warm dark road.

Everyone in our party waits, smiling and gesturing
          with the whole clan, surrounded by snoring
                    black bodies taller than our chins. We squat
                              beside their lanterns, stand inside our headlight.

The driver, who grew up in this valley,
          speaks two dialects, four national languages, plus English,
                    cannot understand a single word anyone says.
                              Solid gold bangles, thick as bagels;

diamonds so large and rough they look
          like large cubes of clear glass. The women stare through
                    their bright syllables. Then one lifts her hand, points
                              at one of us—says something—and they all laugh.

The calf is born dead. A folded and wet black nothing.
    It falls out of its mother—still—onto the ground.
        We watch it in the headlamps. Empty fur sack.
            A broken umbrella made of blood and bone.

The mother tries to run. Several men hold her, throw
    broad coils of ropes around her hooves. Two men, barefoot
        in dhotis, grab her on each side by her horns. And wait.
            They wait through her heaving. They sing

to her, they coo. Men who are midwives.
    Through four translations, they say it is her first time.
        She must turn around and see
            what has happened to her, or she will go mad.

We wait with the whole tribe, wait with the whole night, wait
    for her to stop bucking. Her hip bones
        are as tall as my eyes. Her neck is a massive drum.
            They do not force her, but they will not let her run.

She is pinned to the mountain, her black flat tail points down
    toward her dead newborn. There are four hands
        on her wide horns; four more hold the ropes
            surrounding her haunches.

Finally, after half an hour
    of bucking and grunting, she drops her eyes
        and gives. She lowers her face into it—into the black
            slick dead thing folded on the ground—

and sniffs. Nudges the body. Snorts.
    Then they let her go. She runs off, back
        into the snoring herd.
            Disappears.

IV.

One day, ten years later—one fine, odd day—suddenly
    I will remember all of this. That night, that dark
        narrow road will come back. Like a small sleepy child, it will sit
           gently down inside my lap and look up into me.

Kohl and camphor around all the babies' eyes
    to keep evil away; that exquisite smell of men
        and sweat and dust; the unanticipated calm
           of standing within

an enormous herd of sleeping water buffalo, listening.
    To spend your entire life—out of doors—walking the world
        with your whole family and neighborhood. To stay
           together, to leave together. *What a blessing*, I think,

and then, *What a curse!*
    My newborn is asleep in a red wagon
        that says *Radio Flyer.* I have packed
           a large suitcase and one box.

The World wants to know
    what I am made of. I am trying
        to find a way
           to answer Her.

I place our things by the door. And wait.
    Standing. Eyes closed. Looking. I want to
        remember the carved angels flying over the tall bay
           windows; the front door's twelve perfect squares

of beveled glass; the cloud-high ceilings;
    the baby's stuffed monkey; the tribal rugs; and the photograph
        of our tent in the desert that one soundless morning, on the floor
           of a canyon in Jordan. All in boxes now.

The lights are on. The house
        is empty. Night comes.
                I smell the giant magnolia blossoms
                      opening.

Once, I thought I was a person with a body,
        the body of something peering
                out, enchanted
                      and tossed.

The baby wakes. He is almost four
        weeks old. I give him a piece
                of my body. He fingers my necklace
                      strung with green glass beads.

I tie him onto my back and think about the brazen
        dahlias, nursed from seeds, staging a magenta riot now,
                next to the rusty Victorian daybed, where he was conceived,
                      beneath the happy

banana tree out on the back balcony.
        My father's gold earrings are welded into my ears.
                My mother's diamonds are folded
                      into a handkerchief inside my pocket.

And then, as if
        it is the most natural thing to do, I walk
                toward the stairwell, and give
                      the World my answer.

All the way down the staircase, my hand palms
        the mahogany rail, and I think, Once
                this beam of wood stood high
                      inside a great dark forest.

Thick coat. Black fur. Two russet horns
    twisted to stone. One night
        I was stuck on a narrow road,
           panting.

I was pregnant.
    I was dead.
        I was a fetus.
           I was just born

(Most days
    I don't know what I am).
        I am a photograph
           of a saint, smiling.

For years, my whole body ran
    away from me. When I flew—charred—
        through the air, my ankles and toes fell off
           onto the peaks of impassable mountains.

I have to go back
    to that wet black thing
        dead in the road. I have to turn around.
        I must put my face in it.

It is my first time.
    I would not have it any other way.
    I am a valley of repeating
        verdant balconies.

# Mother Church No. 3

KIN KLETSO/YELLOW HOUSE
CHACO CANYON, SAN JUAN COUNTY, NEW MEXICO
ANASAZI RUINS, AD 1125–1130

*for Henri, at 2*

You step down into the Flat World
Then ask me to say it, to explain

How our name can mean both *ancestor*
And *enemy.* Your body begins in four directions.

Here, one calendar takes eighteen years.
I am three. One day is an eyelash.

Your body is a segment of prehistoric road,
A buried stairwell with only the top stair obvious.

We are alluvial, obsidian.
Sometimes the ground swells

With disappointment; sometimes we know our mountains
Will be renamed after foreign saints.

We sing nine-hundred-year-old hymns
That instruct us in how to sit still

For forty-nine years
Through a fifty-year drought.

We climb down through the hole anyway,
And agree to the arrangement.

# verga:

"... women don't want the men to go
into the bush because the women
will only be raped but the men
will be killed ... I have seen a woman who
was caught in the bush by several men.
They tied her legs to two trees while she
was standing. They raped her
many times and before leaving
her they put stones in her vagina ..."

Abshiro Aden Mohammed, Kenya, 2000
Dagahaley Somali Refugee Camp
from *A Camel for the Son,*
by Fazal Sheikh

*Before leaving her they put stones in her vagina*
The men will only be raped but the stones will be killed
The bush caught many men to go into the stones
The stones will be killed by several trees before leaving
The bush tied the men to the trees in their vaginas
Before bush go to trees they kill many stones
Many men will be caught by the trees in the bush
Several trees will be raped by the bush and killed
Only the caught men will be stoned and bushed by the trees
Several men were caught by the trees before leaving
The men will be killed, but the stones will only be treed
The stones put many trees into the men's killed vaginas
By the bush, the trees were raped only several times
Before leaving, the vaginas were seen standing in the stones

# The Wilde Woman of Aiken

ALBUMEN PHOTOGRAPH ON ORANGE MOUNT
J. A. PALMER, 1882

I am not supposed to be
beautiful. I am not
supposed to sit

before the observant eye
of a sunflower. I am incapable
of having a voice

like a robin's singing
of springtime's newborn impatiens,
its balsams and touch-me-nots

crouched so low to the ground.
Vases and I are not permitted
to dally. If I were a name,

it would be *Wall*
*paper.* My hair is made
of a million breathing paisleys.

For five thousand years,
I have listened to you
think aloud about a world

that does not exist.
I am sitting here,
in the open,

and you are there, dripping
beneath your dark
velvet, waiting for the light

to reach you.
I have wondered
where you really live,

why you cannot hear
all the glass inside your syllables
slide off the table

whenever your mouth
opens and is then closed.
The story has not even begun.

The only thing left inside
my hand is my own
quiet hand. I am the Fourth Sister.

My florets stand together
at golden angles. My head
is packed with eager seeds

crisscrossing in spirals
one hundred garlands long.
It's over now.

About my waist, dark
and bright, there is this
satin sash the color of sun

warmed eggplant
still fetching
on the vine.

You
cannot
prevent me.

# The Mothers

We meet—sometimes—between the dry hours,
Between clefts in the involuntary plan,
Refusing to think of *rent* or *food*—how
Civic the slick to *satisfied* from *man*.

And democratic. A Lucky Strike each, we
Sponge each other off, while what's greyed
In and grey slinks ashamed down the drain.
No need to articulate great restraint,

No need to see each other's mouth lip
The obvious. *Giddy.* Fingers garnished
With fumes of onions and garlic, I slip
Back into my shift, then watch her hands—wordless—

Reattach her stockings to the martyred
Rubber moons wavering at her garter.

From:

To:

At last, a dark murderous lunatic
to whom they are allowed to respond.
Here, no one expects them to be strung
up by their necks—dangled—and then left

to be cut down from a tall tree—and not cry.
No law—here—will require them to watch
their families hurled on top of the world's bright pyre,
over generations—without complaint—

unattended by rage's holiness
or the clear mirror of grief. They find some
chalk to celebrate. While one loads, one lifts,
then checks. Just before they ignite the bomb,

they write on its shell—FROM HARLEM, TO HITLER—
then stand back for the camera, smiling.

# Beauty's Nest

JIM CROW WELCOMES YOU HOME
AFTER THE WAR, JUST AFTER MIDNIGHT
GRAND CANYON: 1951

Beauty's nest
renders the body
mute. An elegance
so inconceivable,
it's violent. Extreme. It hurts
the heart to see
something so vast and deep
can also be made of dirt.

And if it can be
of the earth, the body
ponders, might
such a landscape
exist also within me?

The four of you stand
silent, uniformed on its rim,
while the imagination tries
to conceive all the things
it is still too dark
to see.

You jump back
into your wide tan Ford
and begin to drive
again—again—past
all the motels, and their signs,
which, were it not just
after midnight, you know—
and could see—say
WHITES ONLY

# Red All Over

*The politics of frogs*
*The musth of butterflies*
*Elegies of cotton*
*The whiteness of flies*
*Interruptions by snails*
*A lie's guarantee*
*The hope of succotash*
*A chorus of hominy*
*Permission of the persimmon*
*Observations by the spine*
*The pincushion's reassurance*
*The propaganda of a line*
*Cackling from the Bible*
*Orations by the dog*
*The mirror's steady rifle*
*The fig tree's scarlet log*
*Ands and their derision*
*Lending library in the eyes*
*Patois' agnosticism*
*The tongue's chain mail of whys?*
*Lady calling from the ocean*
*Invisible Man on the moon*
*Lindy-Hopping dead upon*
*The ceiling in the living room*
*Girl asleep in the avocado*
*The minstrelsy of the floor*
*Bickering Birds-of-Paradise*
*Picketing the fickle front door*

# Dog Talk

We-be   bo-broke   e-bev-ry-by
sy-byl-la-ba-ble-ble

O-bour   mo-bouths   bo-broke   the-bem
an-band   o-bo-pe-bened   the-bem
fo-bor   ai-bair   o-bor   wa-ba-ter-ber
o-bor   see-beed   o-bor   foo-bood.

A-banse-se-bers,   que-bues-tio-bens,
na-bames,   se-be-cre-bets.   We-be
be-bent   E-ben-gli-bish,
em-bem-bra-baced   i-bit
the-ben   e-be-ra-based   i-bit
a-bat   the-be   sa-bame   ti-bime.

# Let Me Live in a House by the Side of the Road and Be a Friend to Man

I. HISTORIOGRAPHY

In their Heaven, God is a politician
who can't get enough votes
to be the Dog Catcher.

All the bodies we have
missed return, outlined
with fluorescent chalk.

The sun is a big green apple
dangling in a scarlet sky.
Masses of people bind themselves

up onto tall birch poles, to be
pecked at all day by anti-intellectual crows.
All the trash cans have saber teeth.

After school, they snatch and swallow
the slight bodies of brown boys.
If we make it there, our own kind points

us toward the sky's back door.
When we try to escape,
each taxi drives away

from our outreached hand,
suddenly off duty.


But in my Heaven,
there are five sparkling
Chrysler Buildings, and I take you

to the top of every one. God
is a melodramatic comedian who curses
just as elegantly as Richard Pryor.

The angels wear discarded clothes
made from painted and quilted dungarees.
They carry orange and yellow pom-poms

and know how to Cha-Cha. Deep
emerald rivers twist around this City—
not the East, nor the Hudson, but seven Mississippis.

In vacant lots, between
abandoned buildings, cornstalks
and sunflowers grow wild.

On Saturday nights, I make us
egg salad sandwiches, take out
the boat, then row and row.

There is a hurricane, inside
of which our whole world spins.
It's held within

the infinite palm
of a Goddess
who is Lena Horne's twin.

She wears a gossamer headdress,
and her raven-black tresses are plaited
with all the undiscovered galaxies.


And you—somehow you—
are skipping next to me
wearing a silver skirt,

click-clicking the whole way
in five-inch chrome pumps
made of plate glass.

We wonder together
about the history of history.
The Brooklyn Bridge is folded up

inside my pocket. Someday
I will put it on your finger
and beg you to marry me.

Between us, all the words I want
to say ricochet, exhausted, sweating.
When we stride down the street

the graffiti opens its large coffee eyes.
It follows our freckled footsteps—
and hangs there—quietly listening.

I am the Scarecrow, Tin Man, and Lion
combined. My head's a ticker tape of garbage,
I can't feel a thing, and I am terrified.

## II. I.O.B.K. (INCAPABLE OF BEING KING)
### SELF-PORTRAIT AS THE LION

*for Ted Ross*
*(1934–2002)*

inside a stone cast
peering out at the world
whirl by my heart
a bloody oyster brined
without artery or vein
arms crossed
outside the library
thinking up words all day
rarely confessing
the book's first physical duty
to be the mask
that hides the mane

### III. SELF-PORTRAIT AS THE EMERALD CITY
#### NAIROBI, 2009

Is there a street that can anticipate
our tenderness? A corner or curb
that stands still waiting for me?

Where is the road—gilded and broad—
which can foresee our vast inability

not to love? A capital filled with small rivers
of gingered people sashaying silently through
the tinted streets, effortlessly unconcerned

with a certain world and the way it stares
into the mirror, admiring its own genitals.

Even if I were to disrobe and set out, humbly
whispering the questions of my life into my own ear,
I could not make it past the floor beside my bed

before my nakedness was offered as yet
further proof of our natal rage. I know

there are two presidents who seek solace
behind one enormous pewter mask: one
who believes in a verdant coup; the other

addicted to tradition's scarlet singe. I know
neither man has any real power. I know

one day they will become one man
only, and he will climb back up
into his wonderfully colored hot air

balloon and try to take this place with him.
I am tired. I want to leave. I want to believe

there is a room, a space, just one
ethereal molecule that finds delight
in its presumption of our delicate plainness.

There is yet any evidence, but people talk
about it: some odd empty place called *home*.

IV. GLINDA THE GOOD

*for Lena Horne*
*(1917–2010)*

Pray
there is something
like Her, something

hovering above us,
in whose palm
everything spins

Pray
the stars
are all the feelings

we refused to love
and somehow
they have forgiven us

our refusal
to address them
by their animal names

# Summer

Last summer, two discrete young snakes left their skin
on my small porch, two mornings in a row. Being

postmodern now, I pretended as if I did not see
them, nor understand what I knew to be circling

inside me. Instead, every hour I told my son
to stop with his incessant back-chat. I peeled

a banana. And cursed God—His arrogance,
His gall—to still expect our devotion

after creating love. And mosquitoes. I showed
my son the papery dead skins so he could

know, too, what it feels like when something shows up
at your door—twice—telling you what you already know.

# II

## VOYAGE OF THE SABLE VENUS

*And never to forget beauty,*
*however strange or difficult*

—REGINALD SHEPHERD

# *Prologue:*

What follows is a narrative poem comprised solely and entirely of the titles, catalog entries, or exhibit descriptions of Western art objects in which a black female figure is present, dating from 38,000 BCE to the present.

The formal rules I set for myself were simple:

1. No title could be broken or changed in any way. While the grammar is completely modified—I erased all periods, commas, semicolons— each title was left as published, and was not syntactically annotated, edited, or fragmented.

2. "Art" included paintings, sculpture, installations, photography, lithographs, engravings, any work on paper, et cetera—all those traditional mediums now recognized by the Western art-historical canon. However, because black female figures were also used in ways I could never have anticipated, I was forced to expand that definition to include other material and visual objects, such as combs, spoons, buckles, pans, knives, table legs.

3. At some point, I realized that museums and libraries (in what I imagine must have been either a hard-won gesture of goodwill, or in order not to appear irrelevant) had removed many nineteenth-century historically specific markers—such as *slave, colored,* and *Negro*—from their titles or archives, and replaced these words instead with the sanitized, but perhaps equally vapid, *African-American.* In order to replace this historical erasure of slavery (however well intended), I re-erased the postmodern *African-American,* then changed those titles back. That is, I re-corrected the corrected horror in order to allow that original horror to stand. My intent was to explore and record not only the history of human thought, but also how normative and complicit artists, curators, and art institutions have been in participating in—if not creating—this history.

4. As an homage, I decided to include titles of art *by* black women curators and artists, whether the art included a black female figure or not. Most of this work was created over the last century, with its deepest saturation occurring since the Cold War. I also included work by black queer artists, regardless of gender, because this body of work has made consistently some of the richest, most elegant, least pretentious contributions to Western art interrogations of gender and race.

5. In a few instances, it was more fruitful to include a museum's descriptive titles of the art rather than the titles themselves. This was especially true for the colonial period.

6. Sometimes I chose to include female figures I believed the Western art world simply had not realized were black women passing for white.

7. Finally, with one exception, no title was repeated.

*The Metropolitan Museum of Art*
*Employees' Association Minstrel Show and Dance*
*will be held at the American Woman's Association*
*361 West 57th Street, Saturday evening,*
*October 17, 1936*

*I am anxious to buy a small healthy negro girl—*
*ten or twelve years old, and would like to know*
*if you can let me have one . . .*

—MRS. B. L. BLANKENSHIP

# The Ship's Inventory:

Four-Breasted Vessel, Three Women
in Front of a Steamy Pit, Two-Faced
Head Fish Trying on Earrings, Unidentified.

Young Woman with Shawl
and Painted Backdrop, Pearl
of the Forest, Two Girls

with Braids People
on a Ship with Some Dancing
Girls. Our Lady of Mercy, Blue.

Nude Iconologia Girl
with Red Flower Sisters
of the Boa Woman Flying a Butterfly.

| | |
|---|---|
| Kite | Empty |
| Chair | Pocket |
| Book | Girl |

in Red Dress with Cats and Dog's Devil.
House Door of No Return. Head-of-a-Girl-
In-the-Bedroom in the kitchen.

Contemplation Dark-Girl Girl.
In the Window Negress with
Flower Sleeping Woman

(Negress with Flower Head
of a Woman-Nude in a Land
scape)—Libyan Sybil: Coloured, Nude-High

Yellow Negro Woman
and Two Children—The Flight
of the Octoroon: the Four Quarters of

the World, Holding
a Celestial Sphere.

# Invocation

Untitled
Anonymous
Clay

Prehistoric
Cow
Bone

Detail

Of a
Balsarium
Glass Moss

Fragment
Untitled Gelatin
Silver Print

On Paper On
Stucco On Canvas
On Concrete


Apotheosis:

> *Obverse anthropomorphic sarcophagus.*
> *Alabastron eulogia ampulla.*
>
> *Anonymous fragment.    Frag*
> *Ment.    Pavement (Detail).    Pain t*
>
> *On tin—Figure 150, Figure 151:*
> *Strings and black mud.*
>
> *Terracotta terracotta.*
> *Anonymous relief.*

Untitled Anonymous Limestone,
Isolated Ronde Bosse.

Plant Fiber Beads, Red
Abrus Seeds, Solar-Mosaic Wood Plate.

Ointment Vase, Printed Bedspread,
Artificial Hair—Neck

Decoration from a Tunic. Untitled Chewing Gum,
Gold—Gold Repoussé, Anonymous Plaster-Ink.


Salted Paper, Coins, Carbon,
Ivory-Colored Pencil. Graffiti

On the sides and undergirding
Of a bridge. Da Guerre!

O Type accumulated—Figurine 38 felt
Tip monumental relief.


| *Grass* | *Stain* |
|---------|---------|
| *Ivory* | *Spoon* |
| *Berry* | *Juice* |
| *White* | *Pigment* |


Hide.


Heads and Busts
Headless—Footless—Armless

But with a Strongly
Incised Vaginal


Opening:

*Harp*


*Harp*
*With Bridge*      *Harp*
*Lute*

*One-key*
*Xylophone*
*Slit*

*Gong*
*Trumpet*      *Gong*
*Gong*

*Mallet*
*Whistle*
*Rattle*


*Drum*

# Catalog 1:

*Here is your name*
*said the woman*
*and vanished in the corridor*
—MAHMOUD DARWISH

I.

Statuette of a Woman Reduced
to the Shape of a Flat Paddle

Statuette of a Black Slave Girl
Right Half of Body and Head Missing

Head of a Young Black Woman Fragment
from a Statuette of a Black Dancing Girl

Reserve Head of an African Princess
Statuette of a Concubine

Full Length Figure of a Standing
Black Woman Wearing Earrings

Statuette Once Supported an Unguent Vase
Vase with Neck in the Form of a Head

of a Black Statuette of a Female
Figure with Negroid Features

Figure's Left Arm Missing Head
of a Female Full-length Figure

of a Nubian Woman
the Arms Missing

Bust of a Draped Female Facing Forward
One Breast Exposed      Black

Adolescent Female with Long Curls and Bare
Breasts Wearing a Voluminous Crown

Partially Broken Young Black Girl
Presenting a Stemmed Bowl

Supported
by a Monkey

:

Standing Female Reliquary Figure
with Crested Coiffure and Hands

Clasped in Front of Torso, Holding
a Staff Surmounted by a Human Head

Figure Has Prominent
Vagina Bended

Knees and Oversized Head
with Half-Open Eyes

and Semicircle Mouth
That Juts Out

from the Face Some
Fine Scarification

on Chest and Belly
Dark Brown Almost Black

Patina with Oil Oozing
in Several Places

Numerous Cracks
on Back of Head and Hole

on the Coiffure
One Nipple Appears

to Be Shaved Off
or Damaged Black Woman

Standing on Tiptoe
on One End of a Seesaw

While a Caricatured Figure Jumps
on the Other

End

[Two Nubian Prisoners Bound
to a Post] Protome [Probably

the Handle of a Whip
or Other Implement] Oil Flask Back

View Head of an African Prisoner
Statue of Prisoner Kneeling Arms

Bound at the Elbows
Left Arm Missing

Bust of a Nubian Prisoner
with Fragmentary Arms

Bound Behind Funerary Mask
of a Negro with Inlaid Glass Eyes

and Traces of Incrustations
Present in the Mouth

Censer in the Form of a Nude Negro
Dwarf Standing with His Hands

at His Sides upon an Ornate Tripod
and Supporting on His Head

a Small Cup
in the Shape

of a Lotus
Flower

water jar

bowl

ointment spoon

in the form of swimming
black girl

mirror
with handle

in the form of a carved standing
black girl

handle
of a sistrum

a Bes and an Isia dancing
back-to-back

two nails

with Negro heads in relief

head

of a Negro which may have adorned

a pin

mounted in a

ring

bezel

bowl

           decorated with three heads
           in relief

           separated by flat veined leaves
           female puppet with

mortar and pestle
necklace

           with two heads
           of black women forming

a clasp
perfume vase

           head of an adolescent

aryballos

           juxtaposing two heads of Negroes
           cast from the same mold

mirror
with handle

           in the form of a young Nubian
           female standing

lamp

           in the form of

the head

                           of a black perhaps

incense
shovel

                           with a Negro head attached

to handle
a girl

                           with long corkscrew curls
                           round face wide
                           flat nose and mouth

open

                           and jutting forward
                           to form

a spout

inkwell

                           in the form of a crouching
                           Negro Negro
                           seated writing on

a scroll

Heraldic Lion Holding
Between His Paws the Head

of a Kneeling Black Captive
Statuette of a Negro Captive Kneeling

Hands Bound Behind Back
Negro Youth Struggling

with a Crocodile Negro
Youth Struggling with a Crocodile

Negro Youth Struggling
with a Crocodile Pygmy

Armed with a Stick Statuette
of a Black Girl with Her Head

Inclined Toward the Left
Shoulder Dagger with Decoration

In Relief Lion Devouring a Black Head
of a Black Nude Black Serving Girl

Carrying an Ointment
Chest on Her Head

Ointment Spoon in the Form
of a Swimming Nubian Girl

Swimmer Holds Before Her
a Duck Fragment

That Once Formed the Spoon
[Black Swimmers Symbolizing the Dawn]

Young Black Female Carrying
a Perfume Vase with a Necklace

with Pendant Figure of the God Bes
Drawn in Black Ink Around Her

Neck    Plaited    Lock
of Hair on Left Side of Her Head Relief

[The Queen of Meroë Spearing
Captives] Handle or Pommel

in the Form of Three Conjoined Heads
Including a Black Woman Perhaps

Black in the Clutches of a Lion
Black Prisoners Followed

by Women and Children Statuette
Figure of a Young Black Girl Holding

a Perfume Vase in Front of Her Statuette
of Young Nubian Girl Carrying an Ointment Vase

Wearing a Necklace
of the God Bes

God of Joy
and of the Dance

IV.


Standing


Female Figure with Child Kneeling
Female Figure with Child Standing
Female Figure Head
Rest Supported by Seated
Female Figure Kneeling
Female Figure with Bowl Standing
Female Figure with Bowl and Child Standing
Female Figure Seated
Female Figure (Pipe)
Female Figure Undated
Female Figure Mask
Female Rhythm Pounder


Standing

v.

Attendants bringing
Offerings to the burial

Funerary relief
Detail of relief

Carved relief
Grave relief

Vase with painted
Decoration relief

Site relief
Relief fragment

From the tomb (Isis
Receiving the Sacrifice)

Relief
Relief

Relief
Relief

# Catalog 2:

### VI.

A slave carries jar and two dead birds.
Another slave who carries three

fish and a sheaf of wheat
enters a tower.

Askos, a black woman dancing
between a maenad and a satyr, black dancer

beside a woman playing a tabor—
sacred dance performed

during an Isiac Ceremony, Negroid
dancers and musicians overall.


View: a juggler, a black dancer, Female
Offering Bearer Young Female Slave

with Negroid features carrying a stool mask
of a woman shown holding pouch and basket—

or urn—above two geniuses holding garland.
A standing figure of a Laughing Person

wearing a short tunic with large broad nose, thick
lips, and both male and female attributes: his right

arm broken off at the elbow, the left
arm missing completely.

## VII

### THE QUEEN HAS HER HAIR DONE

Attendants with jewelry, sun shades,
and a mirror, move from right to left.

Mask of a Woman with a large coil
of Plaited Hair Mask of a Woman

with her hair in a Small Knot Mask
of a Woman with Her Hair Rolled

at the Forehead and Temples Mask
of a Woman with Austere Hair Style Mask

of a Woman with Radiating Waves of Hair.
Small and Magical Stela Anhydrite Mummy Mask

of a Woman with a Jeweled Garland Shroud Bracelet
richly adorned diadem with rosette gold

and in lay Two Linen Marks from the Tomb
of a Tattooed Woman Sporting Boat

A Cleopatra holding a—?
Cornucopia Attendants moving

from left to right linen,
from mummy-wrapping Aphro

Dite rising from the bath.    I Sis Aphro
Dite clasping a garment

rolled about her hips:
*The Place of Silence*

VIII.

lotus leaves
buds and cornflowers

poppies and grapes
shape and size of relief

raise their arms
dance on tiptoe


in the tomb

in the relief


a little girl sings
with musicians playing

percussion instruments
the floor sweeper leans

his broom against his skirt
in order to free his arms


for prayer

the curve


of the sandaled feet
vividly conveys

the excitement
of the event

:

head of a princess

with alterations

the small relief

a young gazelle

on the arm of a princess

the relief at bottom


a bull

(        ially preserved        )

is led

place

offering        partly damaged

relief in the Center


the beautifully carved torso

The Queen, Who


Her Arms

the food

Piled     a table

part   the relief


         the Center

:

    small relief

in the               from     bottom

shows portion

    Lady-in-Waiting

      ing      translucent

       breasts

her right hand is a scarf

   feather fan

commonly

 royal

  two heads

the uppermost relief left

end of      representation

:

              Angles

    a room       like       heads

       upper most    the two

partly

      small relief

    (*disk*) -shaped

    adorning

          worn

    women

Occasion

      glories    poppies

    cornflowers

IX.

"Her head is that of a Lioness"

"The short mane of a feline . . ."

"The disk on Her head identifies her

as the Daughter of the Sun . . ."

"King Amenhotep III commissioned hundreds

of statues of the Goddess for his mortuary temple in western Thebes."

". . . brought to England in early 1800s . . ."

". . . these statues were exhibited in the recesses of Waterloo Bridge . . ."

". . . and later by Lord Amherst on the terrace

of his country house."

## X.

South Wall

*". . . to your beautiful face"*


North Wall

*"life, all happiness, all food, all provisions"*


West Wall

*". . . as long as the sun exists, your name will exist . . ."*

# Catalog 3:

## THE WOMB OF CHRISTIANITY

### XI. GARDEN OF EARTHLY DELIGHTS CLASS IN ANCIENT HISTORY

Rainy-Night Sarah
is brought to Pharaoh.

Pharaoh gives Sarah back
to Abraham—Wild Men

and Moors. Melancholy Moses
fighting in the Land of the Blacks

where he finds a wife, historiated.
Bible between two captives, three fates:

Fontana dei Quattro Mori Group
of the Elect Group of the Damned.

A god on the left, a prince
on the right. Back to Back

Solomon worshipping idols, black
laborers on the quays

of Venice. Black African figure
at the edge of the canal, miracle

at the Bridge of San Lorenzo, O Lymp!
I, a miracle of the Black-Leg-Birth of the Virgin,

The Black Bride of the Song of Songs—
Black African Diana the Good

Woman of Color Saint Lucy Before
The Magistrate Pregnant

Eva the First
Lady

Chapel of the Miraculous Image
Inside the Gates of Dawn—

Nigra Sum Sed Formosa Church
of the Black Madonna:

Madonna of Succor
Our Lady of Crea

Our Lady of Peace
and Good Voyage Tanned

Madonna Black Madonna
Madonna Bruna

Black Virgin Dark Madonna
Our Most

Holy
Mother of God

:    *Assumption Immaculata Perpetual Virginity Black Chapel Mother,*
    *The Enslavement of Our Lady the Tabernacle Woman of Revelation,*
    *Queen of Heaven of God, Miracle Mother-Mother of God—Patroness,*
    *Your Majesty Virgin of the Miracle Church of the Black Madonna*

Our Lady
of Presentation

Our Lady
of the Confession

Our Lady
of the Rule

Our Lady
of Plain Light

Our Lady
of the Castle

Our Lady
of the City

Our Lady
of the Hermits

Our Lady
of the Visitation

Our Lady
of the Pillar

Our Lady
of Guidance

Our Black Virgin
of Recollection

Our Lady

Star of the Sea

—of Vladimir    —de Lourdes    —de Guadalupe—

Nossa—Nuestra—Notre—Nera—

—di Oropa    —de Atocha    —de Guingamp—

Rublev Black-Madonna    Marija Bistrica

—of Candelaria    —de Liesse    —de-Rocamadour

—of Einsiedeln    —in der Kupfergasse    —di Canneto    —de la Cabeza

—de los Milagros    —de la Merced

—of Argeme    Onze-Lieve-Vrouw van Regula

Loretana    —Aparecida    —de Marsat—

La Virgen Morena de Lluc    —la Encina    La Divina Pastora

de Antipolo    —d'Anjony    —de Dorres del Portillo

—de Guia    —de la Peña de Francia    —de l'école

de Cologne    Nuremberg Black Virgin

Our Lady of Africa Basilica    La Morenata on the Cliffs

of Bologhine in Northern Algiers    —in the Chadaraita given

by Louis XI    —of Saint Jost near Langenfeld Deutschland    —de la Sède

Zaragoza    Black Madonna in the Woods

Above the Streets of Port of Spain    —atop Nui Ba Den

—in Vilnius Lithuania   —Romería de la Virgen   —Senhora Aparecida

—Olho D'água São João Maria   —de Belloc à Dorres—

—de Montgrony   —La Virgen Negra Istenanya de Montserrat

(in Halles-Sous-les-Côtes)   —de Pompéia   —del Pinar

Black Mary Magdalene of Palestine

Black Madonna Czestochowa, Queen of Poland

# Catalog 4:

XIV.

*Gone!*
*An Historical Romance of Civil War as It Occurred*
*Between the Dusky Thighs of a Young Negress and Her Heart Detail*

*(From a Series of the Four Continents Allegory of America, or Parajba en Brasil—*
*Israel in Egypt—View of Rio de Janeiro from the Hills)*

*Mil Años de Creatividad:*


Alabama Sketchbook:
Seated Negro Woman Looking
to the left, drawing

half-length image
of a Young Negro Woman
Wearing a Dress with an Empire.

Waistline and pearl,
earrings and necklace, and holding
a basket of flowers over her left arm, painting

The Slaves escaping through
the swamp, The Slave watching
her pursuers in for e—

Ground Black Woman walking in front
of a Board Fence Background Plantation House
and Outbuildings (or Slave Quarters).

In a Grove of Trees Slave Woman wearing a Runaway.
Collar with Two Children, emaciated.
Negro Man eating Dead.

Horseflesh in the background.
Negro Man strapped to a ladder, Being.
Lashed Slave Woman seen

from the back, her head in left
profile, kneading bread and smoking
a Pipe Parrot Vendor Negress.

Carrying Her Young Slave Woman
carrying Baby and Negro Boy, running.
At Left Negro Man at right, Being.

Held by the collar, two dogs wear
collars, one labeled "Cass,"
the other: "Expounder."

:

The Negro Revenged Negro Man on a Precipice
calling down Nature's Fury on a slave.

Ship Negro Woman seated.
At right, Slavers throwing over.

Board the Dead-and-Dying.
Typhoon coming.

On manacled limbs of
Slaves among the Waves:

Foreground-Slave,
Ship in Middle

Distance: a Black Woman Kneeling
in a Storm, Her Hands Clasped

in Prayer and Her Eyes
Cast Upward.

Nude Black Woman
in an Oyster Shell

Drawn by Dolphins
through the Water

and accompanied by Cupids,
Neptune, and Others.

:

American Gothic Colored Individuals
Along the Road Side Slave Woman with a Chain
On Her Wrist Kneeling Beside Abraham Lincoln
Who Points Toward Items on a Chair

A Woman and Her Dog in the Window
Black Girl Seated on Watermelon
And Holding a Bottle of Ginger
And Baby in Watermelon Crib

Black Girl Standing
Behind Her
A Redeemed Slave Child
Slave Pen

Two Black Overseers
Flogging Two Negro Slaves
One a Nude Man Suspended from a Tree
The Other a Woman

Bared to the Waist and Tied
To a Tree as a White Woman
Observes Head and Shoulders
Of a Slave Woman Seen in Left Profile

A Standing Female Slave Nude to the Hips
With Manacles on Her Wrists
Holding Up a Drapery
And Looking Downward

:

A Negro Slave Woman
Carrying a Cornucopia
Representing Africa

A Negro Slave Woman
Holding a Plate of Tropical Fruits
Including a Pineapple

A Negro Servant Boy
Brings in a Tray
Of Filled Glasses Winged

Female Figure of Hope
Leaning
On an Anchor

And Holding a Wreath
Over an Inscribed Monument
With a Bale of Cotton

And a Ship
In the Background Negro Boy
Holding Feathers in His Left Hand

Pointing to Hope
And a Book
Under His Right Arm

And a Black Man
Holding a Rifle
And Pointing to the Arms

Of the United States
Above to Their Side
Is a Ballot

Box and Behind
Them a Loco
Motive

:

At Auction Negro Man in Loincloth
serves liquor to Men Bidding

on The Slaves while A Slave Woman
attends Two Women Observing The Sale.

African Slave Encased in an Iron Mask
and Collar Slave Children starting out

to harvest coffee on an oxcart.
Negroes under a date palm.

Negro Woman Seated
at a table, facing

left, writing
with a quill.

:

Abraham Lincoln holding
a Kneeling Black Woman

by the wrist
and lifting Her

to Her Feet
Charity Holding

Three Children
one White one Red one Black

with a Chinese Holding
Her Drapery

Kneeling Negro Woman
lifting Her Fettered Hands

in Supplication to a Female Figure
Personifying Justice

Inside a Wreath
Negro Woman and White Woman Shaking

Hands Negro Man and White Man
His Arm

Around a Small Negro Girl
Doing the Same

Inside a Wreath of Sugar
Cane Stems

:

The Mulatress African Woman with Basket Kongo Basket
full of fruit, diamond-sluicing the Drake Jewel (    'Laud

Anum!) Aspiration: the Masque of Blackness—
Work on Progress into Bondage.

Tall Figure Lilith, The Goat Tender of the Colonies,
(A Christmas Gift to Ole Marster and Missus):

*"Merry Christmas and Christmas Gift, Ole Massa!"*
A Black Child Wearing

Broken Chains
And Blowing Him

A Kiss

xv.

When the Woman's Left Ear
Ring is Pulled

Her Eyes Recede
And a Mechanism Rises

Into Place
Showing the Hour

In the Right Eye
And Minutes

In the Left
The Right Earring

Was Originally
Designed

To Release
A Musical

Movement
With the Pipe

Organ
In the Base

:

Negro Woman Holding
A Bow and Arrow and Wearing

A Quiver
Sits on the Movement

Of the Table Clock at Her Feet, a Turtle
To Her Side a Female Lion

Base Decorated with a Black
Hunting and Fishing

:      *"L'Effroi" (The Terror) Full-Length*

Figure of a Negro Woman
Holding

Her Child Over
Her Head

Out of Reach
Of a Serpent

Climbing Up
Her Dress

# Catalog 5:

EMANCIPATION & INDEPENDENCE

XVI.

A Nun Embracing a Girl
     In a Doorway   Water Dancing
    Girl
        Girl Carrying Child

Wrapped in Blanket on Back
    With Two Girls Near
       Dance Rock Girl
         Nearby Girl

Near Well Girl
    Who Stays Home Woman
      Brushing
        Girl's Hair

:

Portrait [Front]
    of Group of Women
        from Montana
            Left to Right

Good Road Girl
    Mrs. Red Dog Grows in Bed
        Old Woman
            Fierce Woman and Dove

All in Native Dress
    The Question Mark Girl
        Girl Singing in the Wreckage
            Girl in Native Dress

On Horseback Four Women
    and One Girl All in Blankets
        on Side of Street Near Wood Frame
        Buildings

:

Portrait
    of General L. W. Colby
        of Nebraska State Troops
           Holding

Baby Girl
    Zintkala Nuni
        (Little Lost Bird) Found
           on Wounded Knee

Battlefield
    South
        Dakota
           1890

:

Girl Tending a Cow
            Black Girl from the Cottingham Suite
                        Girl Writing a Letter
                                    Girl in Partial Native Dress

With Ornaments:
            Black Seeds Calla Lilies
                        Cyclamen Red
                                    And Yellow Flowers

Little Girl in Orange
            Black Girl White Flower
                        Black Girl Dragging White Girl
                                    Blue

Girl Behind Black Door
            Black Forest Girl
                        Girl in a Green Dress
                                    Half-Length Portrait of a Mulatto Girl

Wearing
            A Madras Tignon
                        And Pearls Girl
                                    In Church Girl

In Front of Chalkboard Girl
            Talk Girl
                        Walking Girl
                                    Jumping

Rope
            In Maryland Park Girl
                        Carding Wool Girl
                                    Jumping

Rope
  Head and Shoulders Girl
    Portrait of an Unidentified Girl
      Young Black Girl

from Copiapó, Chile
  Winnebago Girl
    Washing Clothes in a Stream
      Seated Girl with Legs Folded

"Miss Girl" Peasant Girl
  Negro Girl
    Nude Reclining on Couch Girl
      on Oriental Rug Street of the Slave Girls

Literary and Industrial Training School
  for Negro Girls
    A Section of the Girls
      of the Senior Class

Taking
  a Course in Woodworking
    Negro Career Girl
      Ladies' Whipping Girls

Negro Girl Pelted by Crowd
  Potholders
    with Black Boy and Girl
      Eating Watermelon

Young Girl
  with Red, Black, and Green
    Flag Girl
      from Sene  Gal


Little Brown Girl
  Girl Standing in a Tree
    First Day of Voluntary
      School Integration

Lone Black Girl on School Bus
in Milwaukee, Wisconsin
Head of a Girl Wearing an Ornate Head

Dress

## XVII

Scene 60 Blockade
        Rue de la Lyre
                Outside, Day:

Moorish Women
        On their way
                To the cemetery

Moorish Women
        On their way
                To a marabout

Moorish Women Taking
        A Walk Moorish
                Women in Town

Attire Moorish
        Woman in City
                Attire Kabyl Woman

Covering herself
        With the haik. Aicha
                And Zorah Moorish

Woman at Home
        *I am sending you a package*
                *To be picked up*

*At the railway station.*
        Ouled Nayl
                Woman Uled Nayl.

Young Beduin
        Woman Moorish
                Woman from Laghuat

Moorish Woman Pouring
        Her Kaoua Moorish
                Woman Smoking

A hookah:
        *Bon Souvenir* Natives
                in their quarters reclining.

Odalisque Dance
        Of the Almehs. Belly
                Dancing the Dance-Dance

Of the Veil Dance.
        *Don't get bored* Dance.
                Moorish Woman at Home.

Moorish Women
        In their Quarters Beautiful
                Fatmah at Home

In Full Regalia Woman
        From the South Kabyl Woman
                Woman from the Far South

Of the Oran District Moorish
        Woman from Constantine
                Young Woman from the Algerian

South *Oh*
        *Is it ever hot!*
                Moorish Bust

The Cracked Jug in Contemplation
        (les secrets de l'histoire
                naturelle contenant les merveilles


et choses memorable du monde—
        L'emancipazione dalla schiavitu),
                La Danse African in Algerian Costume—

Nègre du Tombouctou,
        Nègre du Soudan, ou
                Nègre en Costume.

XVIII.

THE SWEET FLYPAPER OF LIFE VIRGIN ON THE ROCKS
DETERMINING TRUE NORTH IN THE RAIN

The Bather Octoroon Woman on Giraffe-
Skin breast-feeding the Mulatress.

Untitled Family Negro House along fence.
The Blind Woman Liberty displaying the Arts

and Sciences City of the Dead. Uncle Ned's
School ' Emancipated Slaves Eel-Spearing at Setauket.

The massacre at New Orleans Cotton Pickers'
visit from the Old Mistress guest at dinner.

The Indian Widow Phrenological Head,
an Indian maiden-spirit of the dead, washing clothes.

Forever Free Anonymous Portia ironing.
Untitled Woman at a gate, holding a cat.

Pictures of Southern life: prawn-fishing mummers
and carnival crowd walking outside on the street.

Day-Work-Woman scrubbing Aunt Dicy,
Woman-of-the-Tobacco-Madonna-of-the-Field.

Jubilee Maternal Recruiter sitting at table interviewing
Family Female Convicts seated outside Sing Sing Prison.

I'm-Just-Doing-My-Job-Red-Cross-Nurses handing out
wool for knitting Free-Fall Female Atrocity Victim.

Watching, ex-voto: Miracle of Our Lady
of the Rosary Off the Coast of Brazil

(Float carries The Queen of Strife and is decorated
          with cast flowers and depiction of two twisted bodies).

In came a storm of wind, rain, and spray—
          weary and dissatisfied with everything.

All-Coons-Look-Alike-to-Me
          men and women carrying bricks.

Massacre of Whites by Indians and Blacks in Florida.
          The Mourners bench progress of the American Negro.

The Hampton Albums water, color-studying the butterfly.
          The Old Arrow Maker and his daughter, Untitled Negro Woman,

Building-More-Stately-Mansions Study Hour.
          Rise, shine, for thy time has come, Negro Woman:

An Untitled American Family Interdenominational Chapel.
          Untitled Young Negro Girl wearing long dress

and bonnet, standing in field holding flowers.
          Anonymous Reclining Negress Woman, at rest

(by candlelight-memory)
          in the garden.

# Catalog 6:

MODERN, CIVIL, RIGHT

XIX.

Anonymous speaking at memorial for Four Negro Girls
killed in church bombing in Birming.      Ham.

President Kennedy addressing the crowd: A Red *Boo*!
A Negro *Boo*! Young Girls being held

in a prison cell at the Leesburg
Stockade. Wounded, civil.

Rights demonstrators in the hospital
and on the street-burned-out-bus:

Bronzeville Inn Cabins for Coloreds. Here lies
Jim Crow drink Coca-Cola white.

*Customers*
*Only!*

:

Birth Treat Girl in Red,
The Two Paths:
What will The Girl become?

Preparing for school
and canvassing for votes:
The Breck Girl The New Black

South Uptown Woman
Scolding Her Companion Woman
Leaning on Radio Woman

Selling Earrings
in Front of Car Woman
with Laundry Bag on Top of Head

Two Negro Girls playing
with yarn and knitting
Needle at Harlem Playground

Three Negro Teenage Girls modeling
clothing for the Teen-Age Consumer
A-Go-Go Woman Holding Up

Spoon at Boy with Mask
who is scaring Young Girl
Negro Woman Peeling

Potatoes Girl in Dress with White Collar
New Jerusalem Women's Rifle Team
at Howard University Integration

Crisis Woman and Daughter
with Children and 22 Million
Very Tired and Very Angry People

Women Marching
in Front of White House,
Crows Wait

Along the Funeral Route
Dancehall Queen Doing the Chaplin
Down the Flank

:

Anonymous Do Drop Inn
Blessed Sun Bathing Negress
Rent Day Beauty in the slums—

Clapping Christening Cleaning
Club Women Cooking Class
at the Benjamin Banneker!

The Green Chair People in a line.
Queens of the Boat hear animals dancing,
wrapping it up at the Lafayette:

Wannabes at the White Party
Gold Brick Inn Roseland
Asphalt Jungle.

Female Carnival Ride Primitive Girl,
The Boss pulling your own strings.
Humanity Servant, you're fine, you're hired.

Group Portrait in the Dark Tower:
Picture perfect painted toenails colonnade—
The Annotated Topsy Series, Untitled,

The Cow Jumped Over the Moan.
Let by gones be bygones, Hiawatha Woman
with Jug Grievin' Hearted Full Blown Magnolia,

measuring and pacing Playland—Comrades!
The Sun God and the Poet
swinging in the park.

There were Colored People there:
In the background, The Pimp—
God's Gift–to–Man

(He told her he wanted to
talk to her and she told him
he could talk all he wants to—).

Clara Mae angry
at Her Sister
and Her Husband.

Workers take the lead,
Midnight Benefit Show: The Screw
as Applied to the Cheese Press.

Me and Willie Mae, Ram Man, Tom Boy,
Moose Lady with a gentleman named Charles Bailey,
Models displaying printed leather shoes.

Tom Boy, Love Owl, Five Sorcerers, Seven
Faces of Eve—Little Miami Magic
People. On Such a Night as This

Unidentified Man Woman and Cat,
Unidentified Something
That Ain't Been Born Yet.

*Woman Power!*
She's Black, She's Beautiful
She's Smart, She's Registered

She'll Vote.
How about You?
Now Dig This:

Don't Hate Me
Because I'm Beautiful
Untitled.

Somebody Paid the Price
for Your Right.
*Register to Vote!*

(You Don't Bomb the People)
You Can *Register Now*!
No Reading or Writing

Necessary
Thenceforward
And Forever

Free—*Thought*
*You Might Enjoy This*
*Memento of the Occasion!*

# Catalog 7:

> *And the colored girls go*
> *"Doot, doo-doot, doo-doot,*
> *doo-doo-doot . . ."*
> —LOU REED

XX.

*Landscape, Western Hemisphere (le tumulte noir)*

Spiral arteries in the female body, evidence
of accumulation, empirical construction extending
horizontal form. Delirium wake and resurrection,

landscape allegories, suprematist evasion,
Black City Convalescents from Somewhere.
My irony surpasses all

Others. Have you any flesh
coloured silk stockings, young man?
Still     Life     Wild     Fowl

Death-Witness while you wait.
I embody everything you most hate
and fear: African    African't    an An

Ti-Slavery Meeting Black Tie Cement Ball:
An Opera in Three Acts.
I have special reservations

between me and the rest
of the land there are bars, something
brown, carmine, & blue:

Middle Grey Grey Area—
Greenheads-Brownheads Untitled Brigade
(stadia circulation style in spades!)

Retopistics Troubled Island,
Zero-Canyon typology.
Do you think

*A* is *B*?    *Girl/ Boy?*
Red-Ball Slave-Girl in holiday attire,
Slave-Girl-with-Jade-Doves-Comb-with-Birds

(Phoenix Segregation). Enough
reframing the past—I sell the shadow
to support the Substance Runway.

:     *Dick-and-Jane-with-Me Page Spread*
         *The Upper Room II Flipside Self*


Untitled Female Drinker Figure—
Reclining Silent Protest Parade.
The result of the Fifteenth Amendment Ritual
and Revolution Self Possession.

Invisible Black Russians—girls with guns—
(Lenin watched from the Tower).
This is my life, cutting up
old film. Don't edit

the wrong thing out
Untitled World's Exhibition: Being
the Narrative of a Negress
in the Flames of Desire

(What remains inside
Pandora Mechanical Girl?
Rabbithole? Fingerprints?
Secrets, Tales

of Amnesia?). I see it
every day, The Conscience
of the Court: Woman-in-Interiors, Plate 1
Wedding Night Untitled Venus

looking into the mirror,
the Black Woman asked
"Mirror, Mirror on the wall,
who's the finest of them all?"

The Mirror says,
"Snow White
you Black Bitch,
and don't you forget it,

Sphinx!"

:    *Las Meninas Autoportrait:*
     *As Armas do Império*


Untitled Anonymous Memory
(the Shape of Things)
Old Dog New Trick Boo

Hoo Revisionist Liberation,
Monkey May Flower May Days
Dawn of Ann: The Liberation
of Aunt Jemima Dancing at the Louvre!

Anonymous Mademoiselle Bourgeoise Noire
celebrates with her friends: I'll Be
a Monkey's Uncle Untitled Committee
to Defend the Panthers Anonymous Fairy Godmother

offers some unrequested advice,
letter from a black girl: Free Black
and passive-aggressive

without sanctuary.

:     *Self-Portrait in Studio*
*(Courtesy of The Artist)*
*The Upper Room I*


My grandmother and aunts
Outside of church, Sisters of the Holy
Family. Three seated figures, guarded

Conditions: Firefighter, firebirds, light
In the window—portrait with sunflowers—
Nine-Lives Pageant of Birds
Torchy in heartbeats.

Anonymous homage to an Unknown
Suburban Black Girl. Self-Portrait
With Mingus Helmet Mask:

Untitled Self-Portrait Spirit
Untitled Book Page
Untitled Woman in a Sardine

Can Emerging, Rocking
Mary Woman Wearing a Fish
Hat. Blackware Pot Maiden,
Fétiche et fleurs, lay on top of me.

Untitled Woman laying down.
Anonymous touching her

Breast.

Darkytown Rebellion
Tit for Tat Brooch

Cut—Beat—Burn—
Balance—Consume

The Rich Soil Down There,
The Bush-Shinn Deboning.

You don't know where
her mouth has been!

Blackberry Woman, Seated
(woman in a blue and black dress),

Stars and Fireworks Woman
Feeding Bird Woman, brushing hair.

Bathsheba at the Fountain,
Venus Before a Mirror

(three wishbones
in a wooden box).

Hip-Hip Hooray! Look Away!
Look Away! Look Away!

"They was Nice
White Folks

While They
Lasted"

(Says One Gal
to Another).

D-Man in the water, *Pomo-Afro-Homo* Peacock
of the Sea, the Spirit of the Dead, watches the Message:

Paris is burning the white to be angry, Anonymous.
Your *kunst* is your *waffen*, Anonymous.

Untitled tongues untied, Untitled American
Gothic marginal eyes, still/here, looking

for Langston. The Black Birds on a steamboat,
Guardians of Desire, the singing head:

*Where Do We Come From—What Are We—*
*Where Are We Going?*—Blues.

Black Girl in a stream,
The Waving Girl seen

from anatomies of escape.
Home by dark, over her *le Cake.*

Walk (Economical Love Pussy Control)!
*Tous les soirs Les Zoulous, Stargazer!*

What on Earth have you done
to this coffee, Black Blossom?

*Pour vous, Madame,*
*Paso doble* as I am.

The Aftermath: underwear
window-shopping, Sunday

morning, fireflies
on the water, blue shade—

Silence.
Poise. Prayer:

*Tinted Venus*

*African Venus*

*Dolni Vestonice*

*Magdalenian Venus*

*Ram Mal'ta Venus*

*Venus from Laugerie-Basse*

*Venus of Hohle Fels*

*Venus of Monruz*

*Venus of Willendorf*

*Venus of Berekhat*

*Venus of Lespugue*

*Venus of Hradok*

*Venus of Tan-Tan*


(Thirteen ways of looking at a black girl)

:

*I send you these few lines in order*

*To bring you up*


*On what has been*

*Happening to me.*


—Venus of Compton

(Young Woman and Hope, Holding
Photo of Pearl)

# Catalog 8:

Still:

Life

(of Flowers)

with Figures—

including

a Negro servant.

# Notes

Art hurts.
Art urges voyages—
——GWENDOLYN BROOKS

BAYERISCHES NATIONALMUSEUM, MÜNCHEN

HENRY FRANCIS DU PONT WINTERTHUR MUSEUM, WINTERTHUR, DELAWARE

NATIONAL ACADEMY OF DESIGN, NEW YORK, 1860

MUSÉE DES BEAUX-ARTS DE LA VILLE DE PARIS

STAATLICHE MUSEEN ZU BERLIN, ANTIKENSAMMLUNG (PERGAMONMUSEUM)

MISSOURI HISTORICAL SOCIETY

NATIONAL MUSEUM OF VICTORIA, MELBOURNE REPOSITORY

LIBRARY OF CONGRESS, PRINTS AND PHOTOGRAPHS DIVISION, WASHINGTON, DC

MUSEUMS AT STONY BROOK

MASSACHUSETTS HISTORICAL SOCIETY

BIBLIOTECA NACIONAL, MADRID

MUSEO NAZIONALE ROMANO

UNIVERSITY OF MICHIGAN MUSEUM OF ART

COLLECTION OF CANDIDO GUINLE DE PAULA MACHADO, RIO DE JANEIRO

EGYPTIAN MUSEUM OF CAIRO

NY CARLSBERG GLYPTOTEK, KØBENHAVN

MUSEO ARCHEOLOGICO NAZIONALE DI NAPOLI

MUSÉE DES BEAUX-ARTS, NANTES, FRANCE

MUSEO DELL'ACCADEMIA, VENICE, ITALY

ARTHUR AND ELIZABETH SCHLESINGER LIBRARY OF THE HISTORY OF WOMEN IN
    AMERICA

NATIONALMUSEET, DENMARK

ALBRIGHT-KNOX ART GALLERY, BUFFALO, NEW YORK

UNIVERSITY OF CALIFORNIA, SAN DIEGO

GALERIE NATIONALE DU CANADA

McCORD NATIONAL MUSEUM, McGILL UNIVERSITY

RICHARD MERKIN COLLECTION, SMITHSONIAN AMERICAN ART MUSEUM,
    WASHINGTON, DC

RMN-HERVÉ LEWANDOWSKI, MUSÉE D'ORSAY, PARIS

BLACKBURN MUSEUM AND ART GALLERY, LANCASHIRE, UK

PENNSYLVANIA ACADEMY OF THE FINE ARTS, PHILADELPHIA

UWE SCHEID COLLECTION, MÜNCHNER STADTMUSEUM

STERLING AND FRANCINE CLARK ART INSTITUTE, WILLIAMSTOWN,
   MASSACHUSETTS

JOSEPH J. PENNELL COLLECTION, UNIVERSITY OF KANSAS LIBRARIES

MUSEO E GALLERIE NAZIONALE DI CAPODIMONTE, NAPOLI

ASTOR, LENOX, AND TILDEN FOUNDATIONS

SCHOMBURG CENTER FOR RESEARCH IN BLACK CULTURE, NEW YORK

BIBLIOTHÈQUE HISTORIQUE DE LA VILLE DE PARIS

UNIVERSITY OF NEW MEXICO

NATIONAL ANTHROPOLOGICAL ARCHIVES, NATIONAL MUSEUM OF NATURAL
   HISTORY, SMITHSONIAN INSTITUTION, WASHINGTON, DC

CHICAGO WORLD'S FAIR, 1893

GEOFFROY SAINT-HILAIRE AND FRÉDÉRIC CUVIER, HISTOIRE NATURELLE DES
   MAMMIFERES

NEW ORLEANS PUBLIC LIBRARY

NEW ORLEANS MUSEUM OF ART SPECIAL COLLECTIONS DIVISION

UNIVERSITY OF WASHINGTON LIBRARIES

GEORGE EASTMAN HOUSE, ROCHESTER, NEW YORK

MANFRED HEITING COLLECTION, AMSTERDAM

COLLECTION PHOTOTHÈQUE DU MUSÉE DE L'HOMME, PARIS

ROYAL ANTHROPOLOGICAL INSTITUTE OF GREAT BRITAIN AND IRELAND

BIBLIOTHÈQUE NATIONALE DE FRANCE

WILSON CENTRE FOR PHOTOGRAPHY, LONDON

MENIL FOUNDATION, HOUSTON

MUSÉE D'ART ET D'HISTOIRE, GENEVA

WALTERS ART MUSEUM, BALTIMORE

MUSÉE NATIONAL DU LOUVRE, PARIS

MUSÉES ROYAUX D'ART ET D'HISTOIRE, BRUXELLES

MUSÉE D'ARCHÉOLOGIE BORÉLY

METROPOLITAN MUSEUM OF ART, NEW YORK

MUSEO CIVICO ARCHEOLOGICO, BOLOGNA

BROOKLYN MUSEUM, DEPARTMENT OF ANCIENT ART

STAATLICHE MUSEEN ZU BERLIN, ÄGYPTISCHES MUSEUM

BODE-MUSEUM, BERLIN

ORIENTAL INSTITUTE, UNIVERSITY OF CHICAGO

UNIVERSITY OF DURHAM, GULBENKIAN MUSEUM OF ORIENTAL ART

SUDAN NATIONAL MUSEUM, KHARTOUM

SAN QUENTIN PRISON, SAN QUENTIN, CALIFORNIA

CUMMER GALLERY OF ART, JACKSONVILLE, FLORIDA

DAVID & ALFRED SMART GALLERY, UNIVERSITY OF CHICAGO

SMITHSONIAN AMERICAN ART MUSEUM

YALE UNIVERSITY ART GALLERY

DALLAS MUSEUM OF ART

DAVIS MUSEUM AND CULTURAL CENTER, WELLESLEY COLLEGE

DETROIT INSTITUTE OF ARTS

FINE ARTS MUSEUMS OF SAN FRANCISCO

SMITH COLLEGE MUSEUM OF ART, NORTHAMPTON, MASSACHUSETTS

PALAIS LIECHTENSTEIN, WIEN

MUSÉE DES BEAUX-ARTS, CAEN

MUSÉUM D'HISTOIRE NATURELLE ET D'ETHNOGRAPHIE, LA ROCHELLE

MUSEO ARQUEOLÓGICO NACIONAL, MADRID

SIR JOHN SOANE'S MUSEUM, LONDON

STAATLICHE KUNSTSAMMLUNGEN, DRESDEN

CENTER FOR CREATIVE PHOTOGRAPHY, UNIVERSITY OF ARIZONA

ERICH LESSING CULTURE AND FINE ARTS ARCHIVES, VIENNA

FOWLER MUSEUM AT UCLA

ESTATE OF RICHARD SAMUEL ROBERTS

SEAN KELLY GALLERY, NEW YORK

CHARLES L. BLOCKSON AFRO-AMERICAN COLLECTION, TEMPLE UNIVERSITY

PAUL R. JONES COLLECTION, ATLANTA

HOLSINGER STUDIO COLLECTION, UNIVERSITY OF VIRGINIA LIBRARY

ARQUIVO NACIONAL, BRASIL

BENETTON'S CAMPAIGNS FOR RACIAL EQUALITY, 1989

ANDY WARHOL FOUNDATION FOR THE VISUAL ARTS, NEW YORK

AMON CARTER MUSEUM, FORT WORTH, TEXAS

MUSEUM OF CONTEMPORARY ART, LOS ANGELES

STONE TOWN, ZANZIBAR, TANZANIA

INSTITUTO MOREIRA SALLES, RIO DE JANEIRO

HISTORIC DEERFIELD, INC.

SAINT GERMAIN-EN-LAYE, PARIS

MUSÉE DE L'IMPRESSION SUR ETOFFES, MULHOUSE, FRANCE

MUSEU DE MARINHA, LISBON

MUSEU DE ETNOGRAFIA E HISTÓRIA DO DOURO LITORAL, PORTO

MUSÉE LÉON DIERX, RÉUNION DES MUSÉES NATIONAUX, SAINT-DENIS DE LA
	REUNION

MUSÉE NATIONAL DES CHÂTEAUX DE VERSAILLES ET DU TRIANON

EYES OF THE NATION: A VISUAL HISTORY OF THE UNITED STATES

LIBRARY OF CONGRESS, VAN VECHTEN TRUST, WASHINGTON, DC

STAATLICHES SAMMLUNG ÄEGYPTISCHER KUNST, MUNICH

NATIONAL MARITIME MUSEUM, GREENWICH, ENGLAND

LOS ANGELES COUNTY MUSEUM OF ART

KUNSTHALLE BREMEN

CLEVELAND MUSEUM OF ART

HARRY RANSOM HUMANITIES RESEARCH CENTER, AUSTIN, TEXAS

JEWISH MUSEUM, NEW YORK

MUSÉE ROLIN, AUTUN, FRANCE

FOTO REALI ARCHIVE, NATIONAL GALLERY OF ART, WASHINGTON, DC

YOKOHAMA BIJUTSUKAN

SINT-BAAFSKATHEDRAAL TE GENT

LOCATION UNKNOWN

III

# Frame

There'd been a field, a farm, hobos asleep in a chicken coop,
white people whose dogs chased us every day on our way to the pool.
I never knew what, if anything, they grew. Never knew of a harvest.
Never saw a thing begin as seed, or sow its way to plant, flower, fruit.

There was a shack, I remember that, and an old house with an old lady.
She wore a dingy eyelet dress, and paced her porch dry
carrying a shotgun or a broom. Flip-flops, Blow-Pops, Click-Clacks,
Cracker Jacks, we barked Dog Talk with teeth still muddy and black

from Eat the Peg. Soft lime salamanders, fingers a vivid tangerine;
cow hooves grafted to arid grime; date palms with roots so determined
they sucked up all the water from the other things with leaves. We tore through her
property, a whole band of us, day after day, unaware of the endings

our bright forms would bring. There wasn't just one, but two
farms, across from each other, and another one, long down
the street, past the pool, next to the Victoria Park Golf Course,
where we never saw one colored man walk into.

Farther out, surrounding us, there were other farms too,
which had been worked, but were not working. There was the pool,
a liquor store, an old house, the golf course, a koi
farm, our new neighborhood, the bakery from Hawaii,

then the landing field for the Goodyear
blimp. You could live here for years and never
understand: Were you rural, industrial, or suburban?
We thought we were *home,* but our cardboard

was just slender venture on Negro sprawl.
Before that, it was law: we could not own property
except in certain codes: South Central, Compton, Watts,
where the construction companies were under contract

with the LAPD to tile or tar our addresses onto our roofs,
so when their helicopters needed to shoot,
they'd know—and we'd know too—
who was what and what was who.


Throughout the whole state, every third person
was from Lousy Anna: New Orleans,
Algiers, the West Bank, La Place, Plaquemines
Parish, Slidell, Baton


Rouge. We took pies and cakes to anyone new, but never heard
a sound from the farms. They never brought us nothing either.
No milk, eggs, no butter. It was just clear in the dirt
road we took. Somebody somewhere


was striding in time, but not any of us.
The farmers were lost
and hating it. We were lost
and couldn't care less.


The third farm I remember because I learned to drive in
it, just after they poured the cement, but before they painted the lines.
Shirleen down the street had it, a creamy sea-green 1969
Beetle. My sister was her best friend. Her baby sister was mine.


They were seventeen. We were twelve.
I'd practice in the evening, sitting on the crushed gold
velvet couch in our avocado green shag living
room. I pretended even then—even then—until I could feel it.


My majorette's baton became the stick shift,
cans of butter beans the brake, gas, and clutch.
The lesson came early, but I missed it: Ease
up when you let down, let down when you ease up.


Do both at once and you won't ever stall.
Choke that bitch if she don't start—
but choke her
*sweetly.* I remember when they first broke

the ground. It wasn't bigger than a four-car garage, but we only had one
car, so what did we know about how big a library was supposed to be?
It was the biggest any of us had ever seen—the only one
besides the three fragmented shelves

collecting dust in Detention Hall.
We'd hang off of each other, sucking the meat out of a giant
navel orange, tacky with juice and pulp, and watch
the corner of the old farmer's plot open up warm and ripe for us.

Trees felled, bush cleared, ground smooth. Small lathes of wood
the surveyor had joined with white string stood up straight in the red mud
whispering where our books would be. A neutral sky
blue, my first library card, my name in my hand—and typed!—

a first too. The lines of my alphabet so particular, so firm—
my definition now clearer than the Helen-Keller-mirror
in my parents' bathroom
(I liked the R most of all).

Then. So that I could see a photograph of an uncommon colored body—
besides a burnt body, or a bent body, or a bleeding body, or the murdered body
of the Reverend Doctor Martin Luther
King—Junior—

my mother ordered books, the kinds with immature
titles only the seventies could have produced:
*Famous Afro-Americans,* which had the same amount
of pages as Dr. Seuss.

Our textbooks stuttered over the same four pictures every year: that girl
in the foreground, on the balcony: black loafers, white bobby socks, black skirt,
cardigan, white collar. Her hand pointing. The others—all men—looking
so smart, shirt-and-tied, like the gentle men on my street, pointing

as well, toward the air—
the blank page, the well-worn hollow space—
from which the answer was always
that same hoary thud.

Every year these four photographs
taught us how English was really a type of trick math:
like the naked Emperor, you could be a King
capable of imagining just one single dream;

or there could be a body, bloody
at your feet—then you could point at the sky;
or you could be a hunched-over cotton-picking shame;
or you could swing from a tree by your neck into the frame.

# Art & Craft

I would figure out all the right answers
first, then gently mark a few of them wrong.
If a quiz had ten problems, I'd cancel
out one. When it had twenty, I'd bite my tongue

then leave at least two questions blank: _____ _____.
A *B* was good, but an *A* was too good.
They'd kick your ass, call your big sister
*slow,* then stare over your desk, as if you'd

snaked out of a different hole. Knowing
taught me—quickly—to spell *community*
more honestly: *l-o-n-e-l-y.*
During Arts and Crafts, when Miss Larson allowed

the scissors out, I'd sneak a pair, then cut
my hair to stop me from growing too long.

# Lure

I am not there

(We are not in that room.
I am not sitting on your lap.
I am not wearing the yellow
and white gingham skirt so pretty
Grandmother just made for me
this morning. Grandmother
is not sitting at her sewing
machine, revving the pedal hard
like an accelerator, driving herself
through the needle. You are not alive.
That fifth of whiskey is not empty
inside your pocket.

I am not three.
You are not seventy-nine.
Your fishhook fingers
are not toddling my birdseed
nipples over and over again.
I am not admiring the shine
of my new white patent leather shoes
resting at the edge of your knee.
Your other hand is not digging
inside my brand-new *Friday*
panties Aunt Lydia just gave to me
last week, because she was so proud
that instead of peeing in my diaper,
I'd learned to make it in the toilet. Grandmother
is not still sitting at her sewing machine, throttling
the pedal harder, louder. This is not your hand, your mouth,
your Pall Mall fingers, your fishhooks, your pearl-
handled switchblade. My father is not at work
mopping floors, unaware of me, sitting here
inside your lap. Alligator.

I am not three. I am not
breathing. I am not sitting in
your lap forgetting the body
has feet and legs and muscle
and sinew. And breath.
I am not just staring
at the wall.

Those are not your countless splendid
black bamboo fishing rods still hanging
upright out there on the garage walls.
Those are not the five gallons of salt
water sitting so still and pale
on the kitchen floor, the ones
we collected yesterday at the beach, to help
my sister's skin. We did not climb down
onto the giant rocks. Grandmother
did not tie pretty silk scarves under our chins
to cover our hair. We did not play
Hide-and-Seek with cranky blue crabs.
That beauty of a day never happened.
There is not a two-story giant avocado tree
in your backyard, whom I love more
than life. There is no grass, no
Pacific, no New Orleans, no Mardi Gras
stories for which I long, no boxes Mamere sends
each hot winter, filled with pralines and fudge
and purple and yellow and green plastic beads.
No Hail Mary blessed art thou amongst women—
I am not here.

My skin does not hurt.
My blood will not spill grey
anywhere. You will not find me
year after year. I will not ever remember
a thing. I will not stare at walls.
I will not see you, all my life, peering
at me from around random corners, whispering
something delicious out of a lover's mouth.

I will not dislike the feeling of touch, will not
be repulsed by the look of desire in an eye.
I will not allow my teeth to rot. The metal
implements of the dentist will not smell
sharp like fresh shucked pearls.

They did not send my mother away
when she was a little girl. They did not
put her on a Jim Crow train alone, in the middle
of a war, headed for Chicago, to make sure
you'd never touch her again, and again, for years.
You did not ever touch her again. They did not
*not* kill you. Again and again. They did not
*not* slice your body into fine brilliant offerings.

This is not that feeling that this is my body,
but I am somehow trapped inside
another girl, unable to say or feel a thing.
This is not the memory of another day.
I am not a wet headless footless squirming
thing you dug up from the dirt beneath the red
anthurium next to Grandmother's breathy
greenhouse and twisted onto a hook. I am not
a fresh pink pulsing thing splayed
on a tray my mother leaves
on your front porch
every Friday, dressed
so pretty. Violet. Hibiscus.
Red Bird. Of Paradise.
I am not there.
The air is not
frozen)

any longer.

# The Body in August

Because when I was a child, God would pull me up into Her lap. Because when She pulled me up into Her lap, She would read to me. Because the story She read most was the one I liked least. Because every day She'd open that thin green book and say, This is the story of your life. Because, from beginning to end, there were only three pages.

I believe in that road that is infinite and black and goes on blindly forever. I believe crocodiles swallow rocks to help them digest crab. Because up until the twentieth century, people could still die from sensation. And because my hunger is so deep, I am ashamed to lift my head.

Because memory—not gravity—pins us to this trembling. And when God first laid eyes on us, She went mad from envy. Because if the planet had a back door, we'd all still be there—waiting for the air to approve our entry. Because your eyes were the only time the peonies said yes to me. Because no matter how many times I died, I always woke up again—happy.

Then, last night, after I'd yelled at him for the first time, my new son dreamt we went walking inside the trees. When we came across a squirrel, he said, I'd kicked it. Then the squirrel changed into a thin green book, which we read.

Because when God became a small child, I pulled Her up into my lap. Because when I pulled Her into my lap—to please Her—I opened my blouse. Because Her mouth is an impossibly pink place, a gaping raw cathedral, which She opened, teeth-to-nipple, then clamped down.

# Second Line

*for Henry Gabriel Lewis*
*& for Henri-Raphael Lewis*

And then, one day, you fell and broke
your neck—just like that—while taking a shower.
Afterward, you walked back to your chair
and asked about the length and color
of the weather lady's skirt (It was brown).
When the ambulance arrived, you told them
*Go on home.* You were *fine.* Two hours later
you slumped over. Still, it took them three more days
to realize you'd severed your spine because the whole time
you told jokes and wouldn't quit smiling. *Pull my finger!*


Stoic and stolen so early on, what is it
about veterans of the Second World
War that makes Death require more convincing?
Three months in ICU, a broken neck,
three bouts of pneumonia, eight heart attacks,
a clement stream of steady infections, and yet
there you were—still: eighty-four, in a coma,
batting your eyelashes nonstop and full speed
at the world. Even while dying, you would
not die. So we were forced to kill you.
But then, we put on Ray Charles. And just when
they pulled the plug, he began your favorite song:
*Hit the Road, Jack!* Which you did. You hit it.
Before the song could end, you were gone.
I've never been so proud as I was that morning,
watching your breath Second Line home so quietly.

Except for that day when I first started
my period, and was ashamed. Nobody
would go and buy me anything because
they said it all came with the new messy
territory. But you drove me right up
to the store, said *Stay in the car,*
then came back out with a paper bag.


When you fell, it was the first month of spring,
March thirteenth. That day, I climbed up into the air
and could not climb back down until just now.


So how do you call that body born colored
and male, hunted and used for cog and prey?
Tree adornment? Altar cloth? War fodder?
And still—somehow—came laughter: often
and more eagerly than fear: your one half-good
eye forever fixed and cocked on the wry glint
of the world. When I was four, you showed me
how to play Tonk, and the proper way to throw down
a bone and score with sound. When kindergarten
began, they had to skip me two grades
because you had already taught me when
and how to Double-Down. That's what it felt like
to be Negro me, daughter of colored
janitor you: *pi* was not a pastry.
History was not a book. It was a smell
like damp cinnamon in your blue work shirt.
Starched pants. Union. Crawdad, crab-boil, oysters
shucked and soaking in their primordial
liqueur. It smelled like all of this, and the Vieux
Carré, its thick peculiar cotton air
breaking beneath the sea's sloppy
canopy. It smelled like the last high note
of the market woman's song-sing-song
whenever she cried *fresh strawberries!*

History was the smell of dirty whites
soaking in a hot tub of bleach; and
your first whore (that nice girl from Storyville
who Onc Félix took you to see when you
were a randy gentleman all of fourteen).
History was the morning of your first
communion; marbles and cigarettes pocketed
inside your muslin altar-boy gown;
it was the smell of gunpowder
from the small pistol you hid in your sock
(to protect your brother Lucien—and other
Negro doctor friends—while they tended
the colored Sick-and-Shut-In). It smelled
like a Palmetto tree, like every tree: red
with sap, warm with wonder; and holy
things, which are common and plain:
a brown paper bag; okra by the crate;
the ironing board when left in a room to cool;
my pencil you sharpened with your switchblade
each morning, just before I left for school.
I sensed all these things—the countries you'd seen,
but I had never been. I could smell the world all over you, Daddy.
You gave it to me—a fresh, sharp walnut—pungent and coy.
You cracked it, plucked out its intelligence,
then dropped it in my hand: this deep black joy.

# Pleasure & Understanding

*Raga in an Afro-Dalit Bhava*
*Twenty-first Century*

Lost landscapes within the body—haggard and lush terrains—
   North and South Poles suspended between pleasure and understanding.
Caravans, safaris, flask-filled hunting parties, all end in this solo expedition:
   you alone groveling from pleasure to understanding.


*All is suffering* is a bad modernist translation.
   What the Buddha really said is: It's all a mixed bag. Shit
is complicated. Everything's fucked up. Everything's gorgeous. Even
   Death contains pleasure—six feet below understanding.


Satiated, sweating, the monk lectures the whore,
   "Salvation comes to him who partakes not in sin."
"Well, it's a good thing I'm a girl," she replies, folding the damp bills
   between his pleasure and her understanding.


Politics, prostitutes, love—in that order. Never war's real horror. "Daddy,
   did you ever kill a man?" Dense silence. Then
tears so slow they never fell. Between us, this intricate moment
   electric with measured understanding.


*I exist! I exist! I exist!* grunts the ego, while the Self reclines
   on Her brocade divan, filing Her eighty fingernails.
With Her fortieth foot, She slides him a tray, and says: *Choose!*
   *A chalice of pleasure, or a thimble of understanding?*

Ancient rumor: When Marcellus captured Syracuse in 211 BCE,
    instead of destroying the city, he paused, and left
each building intact. It was said he believed it would reflect poorly
    on Rome were he to have destroyed *All this beauty . . .*


Your desire is like that, Thief: the perfect crime.
    You broke inside, but took nothing except
Pleasure's location within the Temple Understanding
    (But I wanted to be razed. I wanted to be plundered).


*Sringaram*—love; *hasyam*—laughter; *raudram*—fury; *karunyam*—
    compassion; *bibhatsam*—aversion; *bhayanakam*—terror;
*viram*—the heroic; *adbhutam*—wonder; in the tenth century, Abhinavagupta
    added *shantam*—peace. This is my two pence, *tamasha* notwithstanding.


The Lover takes ten steps forward. The Beloved takes fifty back. Sanskrit
    poems sing of how the rose trembles whenever the bee hovers near.
Listen, I have sobbed from pleasure. And I've cackled
    over my own tombstone, carved with: *Understanding.*


*Ghazal* literally means *talking to women:* a Persian form where royal men
    disguised their boy-love in song. We hide too, me and you.
The alphabet's our court. You're a Lady-in-Wading.
    I had a luxurious dowry—once—but now that measure's outstanding.


By the way, here's the page where I'd write you a love poem, if I knew
    anything about love—or poetry! <snort>
But I still remember—that sidewalk, that tree, that night—a tenderness
    so resonant (despite our imminent crash landing).


It doesn't matter who the *I* is, who the *you* is.
    You know who *you* are.
I know who *I* is. You're a Miss(ed) Pleasure—
    and I Miss Understanding.

But, for you, I wanted this to be a backyard swimming pool at dusk,
   lit from beneath—a thick palm above, lemon branches laden with apricot-
colored dates—a place for you to dive, head and hands first, spend the night
   backstroking between pleasure and understanding.


O Harbinger, what you bring is much more lush than spring.
   After the scarcest of light, Myth says you are the season's sign.
But I maintain you are a plea—something sure when we fall under—
   The Beloved's pulsing red reminder—always—to remain standing.

# Félicité

*for my mother,*
*and her mother,*
*and hers, ad infinitum*

Of all three hundred species
          of hummingbirds, only one, the Ruby
                    Throated, crossed

the Mississippi. Somehow
          this matters to me. They can hover
                    in midair. They can fly

backwards. They fly
          five hundred miles straight
                    through, across the Gulf

of Mexico without ever
          landing.
                    Their mouths are hollow

burnished needles. Bright, sharp flutes.
          They sip the nectar of cactus
                    flowers.


When "Louisiana" meant all the land
          from the Pacific
                    to the Mississippi,

a grandmother of mine once owned one
          of the largest plantations
                    in all the Territory.

When "Louisiana" meant Spain,
        she'd been a slave.
                When Spain sold itself back,

she's listed as the sole owner
        of a vast plantation—a plantation
                so large many property lines now form the boundaries

of an entire county.
        Tonight, after twenty-five years,
                I realized I've spent my entire life

avoiding any situation
        that might require me
                to say these words aloud.

From that moment
        I discovered her rotting inside
                a molding courthouse, her signature

next to the plantation's inventory,
        I began to babble
                any words I could think of

in four different languages,
        placing them in the most chaotic order
                possible, in order

not to say these words:
        *The black side of my family*
            *owned slaves.*

Or her signature: *Marie Panis,*
        *femme de couleur*
            *libre—*

Her lover
     was a famous judge
          from Sardinia.

He took great pleasure
     in watching black women
          hanged inside the Square

to musical accompaniment.
     I read this about him once,
          then tried to see her,

brown, sleeping
     next to him, fucking him
          on her plantation, on top of a pineapple

bed, kissing behind his ears
     sharing an alligator
          pear, strolling

through her cane. Maybe
     at some point every hour
          a part of me has wondered

about her—silently
     —though I did not think so
          until just now.

Perhaps she is the answer
     to this sensation
          I've had for years:

that of another body
     hovering inside me
          waiting for address.

What can History possibly say?
     Sometimes I feel a pride I cannot defend
          or explain. Sometimes I smile.

Into the barbed nectar
          of this story I have stared
                    my whole life.

Whenever someone tried to kiss me,
          I tucked her name under my tongue.
                    If someone tried too long

to hold me, I hid her between my legs;
          if they wanted to touch me
                    there, I'd pull out

her name and place the white bone
          under my pillow, hoping
                    she would return, take it

away, leave me
          a glistening
                    quarter.


To her son, Théodule, Marie Panis gave
          her "favorite" slave: a girl named Félicité.
                    They were married.

One of their children, Heloise,
          was my grandmother's great
                    great-great-grandmother.

There is a picture
          I found of her once, corseted
                    in a studio, standing next to a waist-

length pillar, which held a verdant fern.
          But mostly I have wondered: How
                    does one name a slave Happiness?

Happiness had a twin sister,
        Françoise. I don't know
                what happened to her.


Perhaps, she is still
        out there, like us, her throat
                glistening a silent red.

Or perhaps
        she is the only one
                who can still cross the River,

the only one still flying
        backwards, over the Gulf
                without landing.

# Epilogue: "Boarding the Voyage"

*I know that nothing has ever been real*
*without my beholding it.*
*All becoming has needed me.*
*My looking ripens things*
*and they come toward me, to meet and be met.*

—RILKE

By the end of it, I was on my knees. I'd enter a museum, drop to the ground, and ignore the art completely. I had learned. The art itself had taught me. Art made me kneel.

It was my last day in the museum. A new exhibit had just opened, an exhibit of American colonial furniture. I was there to research an Egyptian temple but ran quickly upstairs to see this new exhibit. I knew what to do now: I didn't look at the image. There was no need. Instead, I walked into the gallery, dropped to the ground, and crawled along the floor.

Why would anyone desire to carve the foot of a black woman at the end of a table leg? Why would anyone find it pleasurable to sit upon a chair whose legs, instead of simple, elegant forms of smoothed wood, ornamented with dahlias or peonies, say, had been sculpted into the shape of four miniature black women, their hands extended high above their heads—four miniature black female chair legs—to hold up the sitter? Which kind of sensation did it create to place the backside of one's body down upon a seat supported by eight wooden brown female hands?

:

A small black female carved into the handle of a tool. Miniature black women who could fit into your palm. A three-inch-long black female carved into a knife handle so you could hold on to her body tightly whenever you sliced your daily bread. A palm-sized black woman in your hand when you brushed your hair at night looking absently into the mirror. A spoon handle, a drum, a hammer, a flute—black bodies sculpted into the wooden frame surrounding a heroic painting of a white male on top of a white horse, riding triumphantly into war. Black female bodies ornamenting the tripods, the base of a table, sleeping inside the frame—selling, offering, tending in the background of innumerable paintings. Bending, standing, waiting. Ever a neck or hand or bending face tilting from behind a column over a shoulder from the margin. Bringing the horses, carrying the hats, carrying the master's sword, his helmet, pulling back his curtain, holding a map, holding a glass filled with cool water, offering a bouquet of flowers. And all the countless European stone fountains supported by submerged black torsos holding up all of the World's water. Our whole artistic history crawling with the decorative bodies of black women.

:

In Italy, in Florence, hangs *The Birth of Venus,* perhaps one of the world's most celebrated paintings.

The goddess Venus stands naked inside a tremendous scallop shell, gliding along the waters, riding the shell like a vessel. It is her *birth*, but instead of coming to us as an infant, She arrives as an adult woman, fully formed, skin whiter than marble, golden tresses gathered together in one hand like endless blades of curling sea grass. Instead of her pointing to her breast, She places her other white hand delicately over her heart. She is attended by two gorgeous gods, a redhead and a bronze-colored brunette. They blow her shell toward shore. Pink flowers with lush red centers fall from the sky like morning rain. As they hover above Venus's shoulder, the whiter god wraps his arms and thighs around the darker one, as if not to fall out of the sky.

In the background, there is an outline of a shore. In the foreground, another female figure, also white, but this time with darker hair—this time fully dressed—awaits Venus's arrival. She holds open a brocade floral tapestry with which she gestures to cover the Goddess's nakedness. The wind bellows inside of everyone's garments, creating the sensation of motion, and hence perhaps more than all the above, Botticelli's painting of Venus is actually Time's portrait too. Like a photograph, Time stands, captured, static, a statue.

When I was a child, looking upon this Venus, I would think that predictable thought: *I want to stand inside a giant shell. I want red flowers to fall from the mouths of clinging angels. I want to hover in the heavens too.*

But what I didn't know was that the original models used for earlier paintings of Venus were Alexander the Great's mistress Campaspe as well as an Ancient Greek courtesan named Phyrne. It's just ancient gossip, but apparently Phyrne was so rich that after Alexander the Great destroyed the walls of Thebes, she vowed she would rebuild every brick, but upon one condition—that an inscription be engraved upon the new wall's face for everyone to see:

*Destroyed by Alexander, restored by Phyrne, the Courtesan*

It's a fantastic story, but what a lush world our psyches might have become had we known the Goddess Venus, the ultimate emblem of female beauty in the Western world, was originally modeled after a mistress and a whore.

:

One day—a banal day of phone calls, cleaning, walking, fetching a child from the playground; watching that child go down the slide, as you stand there wondering, *How many more years will I be standing here at the foot of a slide watching life glide down?*—you turn the page of a book, and there it all is, an engraving:

*The Voyage of the Sable Venus*

Here, the Goddess is not white as marble. Instead, She is a celestial black. And not only that, but She is standing where She has never stood before—throughout thousands of years of Western art: right in the middle of the canvas. She is not just a torso, or head, or scrap of a face. She is not holding a service tray or selling fruit or hanging from a rope. Like her sister in Italy,

She is poised atop a seashell: a black goddess gliding along the waves of a primordial ocean, balancing inside a giant scallop shell. In other words, the beginning of the world.

The strapping and cut boy-gods in Botticelli's painting have been replaced, however, and here She is attended by white cherubs, most of whom fan the Sable Venus with long white ostrich plumes. A few carry the feathers of a peacock. Cupid, above, takes aim at Triton, below. Triton glides through the waters, navigating Her shell. Oddly, he does not carry his usual trident, but rather holds a flag—a flag of the Union Jack.

Botticelli's definite horizon is muddled here. Where is the land? Indeed, where *will* they land? They are all riding across the middle of an ocean, shepherding the Sable Venus to some (as yet) unclaimed place. Perhaps her body will be used as a land claim, a territorial marker, a stake, a fleur-de-lis.

Instead of pointing to her breast, like the Virgin, or covering her breast or heart, like Botticelli's Venus, the Sable Venus has a pair of reins threaded through both of her hands. The reins are harnessed to two dolphins, dolphins that pull Her chariot-shell through the sea. Unlike Botticelli's pure and naked Venus, the Sable Venus wears one article of clothing: a pair of what can only be called colonial panties. And unlike Botticelli's Venus, the Sable Venus is strong, curved, muscular: a woman's woman. Her form is twice as wide; her muscles cut, lean. She is the embodiment of strength—no fragile anything in need of anyone. Her dark skin is adorned with jewels. All eyes are upon Her and at Her service—finally.

:

At the time when She was first rendered as an engraving by Thomas Stothard in the late eighteenth century, and later painted in 1801—and still today—*The Voyage of the Sable Venus* could be considered a visual travesty, an inversion of order. *How, at the height of slavery, could a black woman be drawn by dolphins through the primordial seas, adored and attended by the gods and angels of Classical Greece?* goes the purist response, meaning the gods would never be seen in the company of a black female body, not to mention serve as her attendants. Others, recognizing immediately the atrocious irony, still question whether the painting was a satire. For in the eighteenth century, Her scallop shell could only be a metaphorical slave ship.

Did the Sable Venus enjoy her trip across the Atlantic, guided by a white male celestial harem, gliding along the Middle Passage, destined for slavery?

:

Besides these obvious observations (that the world was on fire then; indeed, that it is has been burning for millennia; and not only that, but that the majority of our population seems to be enjoying the blaze), you begin to feel a third question about the image rising in your throat, a subtler question about words. That is, you begin to wonder if you had ever seen the words *Sable* and *Venus* in the same sentence, at any point in time, in any language, anywhere, in print.

Just think of it: a word as exhausted and underinvestigated as *Venus*, had you really never seen it occur intimately with something dark and adjectival?

Of course, the answer is, tragically: *No*.

But there was something else at play, something not so predictable or boring as hate. Something hid beneath the floorboards of your question, eyes peered up at you through the cracks in the question's floor: perhaps for all of these centuries, for all of these thousands upon thousands of years, the *true* reason no one has never seen *Sable* and *Venus* in the same room together, at the same time, is that, quite simply, they are the same person.

The Goddess Venus a double agent with two code names—
one: *Darkness*
the other: *Beauty*.

:

When I was a child in the first grade, I began making female statues from mud. I don't know why.

*mud*

*clay*

*strings*

I dressed the statues in repeating rows of red papery bougainvillea petals, ornamenting each "seam" with bright gold pistons I'd plucked from the center of our neighbor's fuchsias, sometimes adding a violet crown with pistils from the heads of the Birds of Paradise that stood erect guarding our front door.

I would play a game. I would write a very short note that said only *Love*, then leave the note with the wet and ruddy statues, anonymously, at the front doors of the old ladies in our neighborhood.

*Ding-Dong-Ditch:* ring the bell, then run.

:

Of love's mysterious arrival, Rita Dove wrote that the occurrence is "massive, inconvenient, undeniable."

How like love art can be. A painting can have me at hello. I have gone out on dates with certain sculpture. I can court a photograph for lifetimes, waiting for her to marry me.

But art's seduction needn't be dramatic. In fact, sometimes it is as quiet as a drop of sweat silently tracing a downy line of hair down your back. Like love, we barely notice certain aspects of art until hours later, when we wake with our clothes drenched.

At other times, art takes us by the throat. It bends us. And we like it. Finally, something capable has claimed us, tamed us. If the art is good, it forces us to stay. Exceptional art, like exceptional love, forces us to cry out for mercy.

:

Which is to say, I fell in love with the *Sable Venus* at first sight.

It wasn't merely the iconicity that grabbed me by the neck. Nor was it that deeply satisfying delight in seeing the white Venus replaced by the black. As delicious as that is—*and it is!*—that gesture was too undemanding, of myself, of History. Which is to say, ever since Rome, we keep replacing the statues but continue playing the same blinding games. *Hey, I have an idea!*

*Let's take down one monument and replace it with another! That will fix our problems!* But what if the real neurosis stems from our desire for monuments of any kind? Perhaps instead of looking up for an icon, we need to look down and cherish and adore, even worship, the people working quietly right beside us, or even more subtly, working—via memory—right within us. Real beauty isn't tit for tat, as fun and even justified as revenge can be. So *The Voyage of the Sable Venus*, for me, was more than a visual sleight of a historical hand. That *something more* was the title. *The Voyage of the Sable Venus* was an epic written in one line.

:

Frost Medalist Marilyn Nelson once remarked that if one has the ear and takes the time, even the front page of the newspaper is laden with sonnets. The back of a cereal box contains songs. Language is an organ, a musical instrument. Which means that even when having an argument, we are singing.

The title—*The Voyage of the Sable Venus*—contained the story of all our histories.

Could it be, I wondered, that instead of the intellectual propaganda we call *Art History*, the more honest, simple, and accurate narrative of art, of perception, of projection (in short, the development of our visual subconscious), was hiding right there in plain view—not, however, in the imagery, but simply in what the image is called, within the signs, within the words?

Whenever I had walked inside a museum, had I missed the obvious treasure because I'd been seduced into looking at the paintings?

Inside the title of any work of art, armies stand. Horses, canons, five-masted ships anchored in the harbor, the general watching Death dance from on board. How had I missed it?

Is it possible that titles can contain more art than the image itself, even titles like *Anonymous* and *Untitled*? Perhaps silence is the greatest epic of all.

Or, as one of my favorite and most astute cultural critics, Richard Pryor, once asked, "Are you gonna believe me, or your lyin' eyes?!"

I had to see.

I needed to see how I had been *taught* to see.

I decided to go back.

I decided to start my life over.

:

If we considered an art title the true portrait, the hidden image, what would we see?

If we refused to look at the painting, could we perceive more of the art?

Which story, which music, would emerge?

If Darkness and Beauty were the same agent, had she hid in other titles too?

If we went back, if we went all over the world and looked at every object, every statue, every painting that included a black female figure in any way, and wrote every title down, what would art's epic sing then?

What recitations, repetitions, recollections? Which suites, what alliteration, rants, odes, meter, anaphora—which fixed and unfixed forms?

Is language really a textual code, or a visual one? Or is it both? Could a title perform like a painting? Is this a possible answer to that eternal unanswerable question: What is a poem? And that question's hidden twin: What is an image?

:

I never thought I would find more than just a few titles. I never thought I would travel through time. But after I began to write down each title, what began as a small experiment expanded into the history of art in the entire Western world. The museums were invisible graveyards. They were just sitting there: broken, defaced, unseen. A catalog of bodies.

It was an invisible archeology—an archeology that crisscrossed time and space. Everywhere I went, I found them, just off, just to the edge, just beneath: pieces of black female bodies buried in plain sight.

We were everywhere.

:

Over the years, my project stopped being *research,* and I began to feel that although I lived in New York, and although I was a mother with a three-year-old son, carrying four bags of groceries while hauling him and his stroller up four flights of stairs, mashing him bananas and avocados during the day, there remained, nevertheless, a vast part of me that was leaving to serve on board a great ship only I could see. It just happened. One evening, as my son slept in his room, a Head Start neophyte overjoyed with new toddler high society, it felt to me as if a vast and ancient ship berthed itself in the middle of our block, right outside my window in the East Village, on Ninth Street. Long before Hurricane Sandy would wash into our lives, flooding our building with nine feet of water—that is: a year before someone's white leather sofa went floating down our street at two in the morning—I had already seen our block transformed into an ocean, and that ocean held a curious vessel that I knew had come only for me. The captain of this ship was the Sable Venus herself, and She gently demanded that I get on board.

More than a boatswain, but always honored to be in Her service, I understood my job was no longer academic, but something more open, more catholic, in the truest sense of that word. *Why me?* I wondered. Sometimes I thought it was because I was the one who had the most arms, the only one whose legs still worked. Unlike the Sable Venus, I could actually step ashore, walk undetected inside museum doors, and begin the long catalog of our beloved missing, our cherished disappeared. Sometimes I understood I was allowed on board because—for me—this was the most exquisite and most perfect place in all of History to be. Voyaging through time and place, our ship a nautical temple, a haven from a war fought not over any geographical territory, but the greatest ideological territory of all: *Beauty.*

It was as if when I said I had to start my life over, the Sable Venus had heard me, and She had come.

:

The first days, when we were alone, just the Sable Venus and me, She would dock our ship, and I would get off in Ancient Greece, say. Or I would get off in Colonial Williamsburg. In each port, I'd go on shore and begin searching—in museums, in libraries, in archives, in courthouses.

Black female figures were everywhere. That was the first shock. As far back as 38,000 years, as far away as any port, any continent, and in every artistic medium ever practiced. Quite possibly, the black female figure was as old as pigment itself.

In my real life, I'd take my son to museums several times a week. I spent my first Mother's Day with him strapped to my back at a Kara Walker retrospective. He was a just a few weeks old at the time, and the black and white silhouettes astounded his new eyes. I took him with me on airplanes, trains, a small ferry across the Lamn Archipelago. Wherever we went, I visited museums. I wrote down every title I could find. After countless exhibitions, countless books, countless archives, I had collected thousands of titles. Any art object that contained even a fragment of the black female form, I wrote down. Maritime museums, train museums, weaponry museums, courthouses.

*History* was the sea upon which I grew drunk.

My duty was to find them, to find each one, to bring the broken bodies aboard. I hid the sculpture in my hair. I hid the paintings in the baby's stroller. I became a very accomplished international art thief. It was easy. By writing down the titles only, I was able to steal all of the art by leaving it there. I'd write down the title in my notebook, bring her aboard, wrap her in blankets, clothe and feed her. By the end, the ship was full. A catalog of dismembered and dead. Burnt, broken, chopped, half-length black female bodies. Torsos, limbs, often standing, unable to sit, without relief—frozen by their artist in a position of eternal servitude. In short, the most capable of all shipmates.

There were so many black female bodies aboard, after a while there was nowhere to walk or sleep. I cooked for them. I'd hold a figure with half of a face—no arms, no legs to speak of. I'd sit with her. I worked silently so I could eavesdrop on their conversations. The paintings talked to each other. The sculpture talked too. Often the only body they had was a head peeking out from behind a column. I looked deep into their bodiless eyes. I poured broth inside their mouths.

:

*Untitled Untitled Untitled Untitled.* Hundreds of thousands of female figures of every race in Western art are titled simply *Untitled.* Double that are named *Anonymous.* You could write the word *Untitled* repeatedly on a piece of paper every day, all day, for the next one hundred years without stopping, and you'd never reach the end of female namelessness.

I began to grow wild inside. I felt as if I were always on board, always at sea. I'd be sipping tea with a friend, but really I was standing on deck quietly watching the sharp horizon. Almost every figure on board was broken in some way. Everyone was dead, but the ship became a party. Brokenness, fragmentation was a given, if not our most enduring strength, if not our anthem.

What could anyone whole or alive truly know about living?

:

It was an exercise in the redemptive power of silence. The art challenged me to stop speaking. The titles were adamant that our opinions and theories about art were wholly unnecessary.

I tried "to write about it." I tried to write something else. I tried "to write" more, to say something about how it feels to be on your knees in a museum with a magnifying glass, to be under suspicion by the museum guards for doing nothing other than looking more closely.

I tried to write about the hysterical laughter that would project from my mouth in the middle of the night as I discovered yet another unbelievably heinous art object, so sick the modern mind could never have conceived of it. Each time I tried to write *about* the art itself, I would find yet another image whose title, shockingly, could say more about human beings in a few words than any art historian, writer, or artist could accomplish in a million pages, with a million images.

What more was there to say? What could possibly be said?

Perhaps the true museum, the most honest archive—the eternal exhibit—occurs and reoccurs within our own bodies. Perhaps the gallery is not material but memorial.

Like Rothko's Chapel, every image exalted in darkness.

Or as Roland Barthes once said, "A photograph is always invisible: it is not it that we see."

:

When my son grew too large to carry on my back, I began to travel from my bedroom while he slept. Sometimes, because of the new forms of wireless access, I'd break into my favorite museums by going to an online exhibit. I'd go roller-skating through the Met at two in the morning. I'd sit at night in the Temple of Dendur. I'd eat a bag of barbecue potato chips and offer some to the Mona Lisa. Matisse and I became wild lovers. I two-timed him with Laurette. But then the ever-suave Gordon Parks stole me away from her in two moves.

Or maybe we were more like a ship of black female pirates, and I was the only one who could pass. I was cursed, you see: I had a whole face. But we used my body's wholeness to our advantage. I could get in; I could get past the guards. And perhaps that is why they chose me. I grew my hair long like black sea grass. Friends thought it was because I wanted to be glamorous, but the true reason is I could hide my invisible tools and weapons near my scalp. Looking so much like what women are supposed to look like—long-haired, pushing a bourgeois $500 baby stroller—no one suspected me of my true calling: thievery.

We went all over time because we *were* all over time. History was a tunnel or a river or a lane. History was a sky full of stars. History was a rope, a gate, a laboratory run by the deranged. History was a compass.

By the end, the ship was full of fragments. A catalog of dismembered and dead—burnt, broken, chopped—half-length black female bodies. Which is to say: the most capable of all shipmates.

:

Every day, every hour, there were countless surprises. My eyes changed colors: sepia, onyx, tar, tiger's eye. I began to cackle to myself. Western art seemed to hold a long black secret. And I could finally see it.

Beauty isn't pretty. Beauty and pretty are enemies. Pretty is a Yes Man, dressed in colonial drag, passing for a lady. While Beauty is a double agent. Beauty is a war cry. And Her first commandment is to stay well hidden.

:

I no longer look at beauty straight on. I no longer look where the painter has guided my eye to gaze. I tilt my head. I turn my body to the left and try to discover Her strange existence from my periphery. At some point I blur my eyes.

:

Or perhaps *Voyage* is a kind of autobiography, an autobiography without an *I*. For as Virginia Woolf once said, " 'I' is only a convenient term for somebody who has no real being." Or *Voyage* is an autobiography where the *I* isn't significant, isn't the protagonist. Perhaps History is both hero and villain. Which is a kind way of saying perhaps History is that lover I both hate and adore. I cannot quit Her.

:

And then one day, perhaps because She sensed that I was finally beginning to understand what had taken place, or perhaps she thought I was starting to turn mad, or perhaps she realized I was enjoying too much being with the dead, the Sable Venus turned our ship toward Christianity and the medieval period.

Naturally, as we turned into the harbor, I expected there'd be a rash of flotillas racing toward our ship for refuge, flotillas populated with black, broken figurines, clamoring for escape. I thought we would be able to sense the sadness and despair before we even dropped anchor. I thought of all the dark women's bodies compromised or burning in the genius mind of Hieronymus Bosch. I thought there would be shouting and calling out. Cacophony. But instead there was only silence. I looked toward the Captain—My Captain—but the Sable Venus only smiled.

:

It didn't make sense. Wasn't this the religion where a man believed to be a god had been sadistically murdered, then left on a cross to bleed?

Christian art held a black, feminine visual silence.

It was as if, suddenly, all of the horrific visual gestures toward black female bodies that had occurred in the ancient world suddenly just disappeared when we arrived at Christianity, as if the history that had preceded us had never really taken place. We went from this intense ancient saturation of complete racial and gendered degradation—utterly bizarre, illogically pathological—and then suddenly, relatively speaking, there are no images of black women during the art of Christianity. Besides the Three Kings who visited the manger, and a few counts here and there who had married a few black royal wives, the Christian period seemed to suggest visually that black women quite simply had rarely existed.

I could not accept it. I was perplexed. I grew enraged.

There I was with a magnifying glass, groveling along on my knees again through History's arduous corridor, spending every hour in the museum looking down, to the edge, to the end. I had begun to study paintings of the manger, of the Annunciation, of the day that Christ was born. I found mice running beneath sacks of wheat. I found endless white maids carrying countless jugs of milk, of water, but with the exception of the art of Hieronymus Bosch, where it is difficult to know just who is what, I found little evidence of the black female figure.

And then one day, as I crawled around from manger to manger, finally the Sable Venus whispered to me, *Get off the ground. Look up!*

:

And there She was—not a maid, not a servant, not fractured or broken in any way. Indeed, for the first time in Western art the black female figure was completely untouched by any hand, ever. There she sat, glowing, inside the manger, with a halo whose light encompassed the whole room, as She held her only child, the Christ, the son of God. Holy Black Virgin, Mother of All the World.

:

I had grown so accustomed to the ground. I had accepted, in a delicious way, that the richest place to be in Western art was on my knees, on the outside, out back, even underground. I had crawled all around Her manger without ever noticing She was sitting right there. The Black Virgin smiled at me. She stroked my cheek. She offered me her velvet brown hand and insisted that I stand up.

I had not been able to find Her because I had been looking only in museums, only investigating objects that were dead. But the Cult of the Black Virgin is one of the largest *active* goddess cults on the planet. Her image is worshipped by millions of Christians throughout the world. Like the Venus figurines, there are countless Black Virgins standing high up on the altar on every continent, on every island, in every city. You can't find Her inside a museum because She is too busy being worshipped and adored. You have to visit her temples, the various churches throughout the world that have no time for mere observation because they are better occupied with Her adoration and protection, century after century.

She is on top of a mountain in Vietnam. She is in a church on a roadside in Palestine. She is in a small chapel in Tobago. She is everywhere in Mexico. And Poland, perhaps even more than Italy, has guarded her with its life, offering her refuge and devotion, war after war.

And so our ship stayed in Christianity for a while, not because there were more paintings to find, but because—ironically—staying beside the Black Virgin was the only place in Western history where we found we could rest.

:

During the Victorian period, painters discovered a pigment that would help them to paint brown and black bodies more realistically. It was called *Indian Yellow.* The yellow was so rich that it created a more lifelike depth in brown skin. Until that time, no one really knew how to paint black bodies well. Our skin appeared strange, without depth or contrast. Indian Yellow was a visual sensation. It changed completely how brown bodies were rendered.

Slowly, over time, the origin of the color fell under suspicion. Was it really plant-based? What made the yellow so rich? And although guarantees were made that the source was indeed vegetable, it turned out that Indian Yellow was made from the urine of cows, cows in India that were being force-fed a diet of mango leaves only. The cows would of course die after two years.

There was outrage in England. "How could anyone treat a cow so cruelly?" went the questioning. This case spawned the beginning of animal protection organizations in England, decades before anyone complained about the slaughter and devastation the British Crown was inflicting on India's people.

:

I often think about Thoreau and Walden Pond. I regularly feel as if I am a pastoral poet trapped inside a postcolonial body. I contemplate all the miraculous flowers, trees, and grasses; animals and birds; all the exceptional life just throbbing and teeming outside my window. I think about how we would have no vegetables, fruits, or flowers were it not for the great pollinators: bats, butterflies, bees, hummingbirds, the common housefly. I think about maggots and worms, how holy is the work they perform. But just as I am about to transcend history entirely, I remember Thoreau, who—no matter how hard he tried to find a place of natural peace and beauty, a place where he could escape history—kept bumping into former slaves and free black people living around Walden Pond.

Which is to say: Western art is our Walden Pond. No matter where we go, just as we bend down to admire the red pulsing veins of a leaf, we bump into History. History is a runaway slave—running, running—trying to find some place to be safe.

:

Besides those routinely murdered on board for pure sport, is it true that on slave ships, in the middle of crossing the Atlantic, before ever arriving in the so-called New World, many, many slaves who died en route did not die of anything mythical, like flying (as the folktales say), or of anything viral, but from something much more insidious and vital, like despair, or what we now call *depression*?

It was common.

There are records.

Perhaps despair is a truer kind of *flight*.

Perhaps depression is a brand on the runaway, an honest imbalance presenting in our blood—a certain enduring and rational disappointment in our species.

Or as Fred Moten once said brilliantly:

> I want to consider exhaustion as a mode or form or way of life, which is to say sociality, thereby marking a relation whose implications constitute, in my view, a fundamental theoretical reason not to believe, as it were, in social death. Like Curtis Mayfield, however, I do plan to stay a believer. This is to say, again like Mayfield, that I plan to stay a black motherfucker.

:

Which is to say, when the voyage ended, I was—of course—the last one to know. I am convinced every figure on board knew our time was ending, but each agreed to conceal that fact from me. Again, perhaps I was enjoying being with the dead too much. Perhaps while documenting their slivered testimonies about how they came to be just a dot of a woman standing off to the side of a canvas, or a table leg, or fragment of a figure, I myself was turning into a statue.

Perhaps, in my postmodern self-righteousness, I had missed the point completely and believed their brokenness was the subject, when what became most clear, after sailing for several millennia, was that their armlessness, their facelessness was not the problem all. The problem was the notion that they were not alive, that they did not exist, that they were not right there in the painting, looking right back at you. *Las meninas.*

Or as Christa Wolf once said:

> It was here. This is where she stood.
> These stone lions looked at her;
> now they no longer have heads.

:

As the ship turned in from the Atlantic, I saw the New York skyline. But when we got to the pier, there was an odd silence. Not the usual ecstatic ruckus a ship chock-full of broken women, recently freed, will make. Instead, nobody moved. No one took any steps forward toward disembarking. They all just turned in silence and looked at me.

It was my turn this time. How could I not have anticipated this?

Instead of going on shore and returning with more images, more forms, I was the broken body who would be getting off and not coming back. I was the one who had been rescued.

:

And then quite simply it was the present. Suddenly, I was walking up the East River toward Chinatown. Suddenly, my son was still asleep in his bed. Suddenly, I was making him oatmeal before school. Suddenly, I was sitting on the subway going to the hospital where I worked.

It was done. A whole ship of them, an invisible ancient ship of black women, a ship upon which I had lived for thousands of years, just like that: gone. I could feel them out there, a massive ship of broken clay figurines; pieces of a canvas; millions of women named *Untitled*; hundreds of thousands of serving girls—women who could never sit—so many arms filled with baskets and bowls bent over in perpetual service; thousands of little Venus figurines; women in petticoats—bleeding; women with parasols; women with the heads of lions or deer; someone wearing a fabulous polyester suit; someone running for president, her fingers open in *Peace!*; someone walking alone down a street, stopping to stare into a window on a Sunday morning. The ship was an Ark—and all of them were singing and cackling.

All I could think of in that moment was Whitman's "Birds of Passage"

> Raise the mighty mother mistress,
> Waiving high the delicate mistress, over all the starry mistress,
>   (bend your heads all,)
> Raise the fang'd and warlike mistress, stern, impassive, weapon'd
>   mistress,
>       Pioneers! O pioneers!

And then Bob Kaufman's

> All those ships that never sailed
> The ones with their seacocks open
> That were scuttled in their stalls . . .
> Today I bring them back
> Huge and transitory
> And let them sail
> Forever.

:

For some poets—for me—writing is an archeological act, an archeological practice without landscape or time.

We stand here floating on the air with you.

We ask you to imagine with us that what we see is true.

We want you to agree to the lie that there is a floor, when we all, each of us, know very well there has never been any such thing as a floor.

We pretend together anyway.

A writer does not wish to lecture you about the past—we want to take you there instead.

Which is to say, we want your company.

The most sincere poets want to hold your hand because, like you, we are also afraid of what we will find—some human horror too heinous to accept alone.

And the opposite is also true: we're terrified of finding finally that Beauty that is overwhelming simply because—in the midst of all these Hells—She actually exists.

A hidden lapis amulet to ward off Death.

I write because life is lonely and I want you there.

I write because all I want is you—here—with me, stepping down into the countless pages of the earth with a small brush in my hand, a lantern in yours, that sound of your footfall on the dirt steps beside me.

Maybe you'll caress my shoulder, just to signal a hello, just to say you're proud, you don't know of what exactly, perhaps the simple fact that somehow mammals are still here fashioning useful objects out of simple elements.

Maybe you'll pull an apple from your bag and hand it to me.

:

There is a disease the French call *mal de débarquement;* in English it is called *disembarkment sickness,* or *land sickness:* an illness one feels after ending a prolonged voyage at sea.

After the trip has ended, one still feels the ocean rocking beneath one's feet. The whole room sways as if the house were floating atop an ocean. You get seasick while sleeping in the suburbs. You never stop hearing the ship's bell, quietly but symphonically ringing the hours of your watch.

There is no cure. Sometimes the only remedy is to get back on a boat, to go back to sea.

Which is to say, some part of me remains tied to Her mast.

:

Still:

How like love art can be. Art stands there before you, full of caresses, but at a distance. As when that hand I have watched for years, studying every line, is finally in the same room, reaching out toward mine.

I do not think of the person to whom the hand belongs. Instead, all I can feel is *Beauty.*

At a dinner party, as I dip something into a bowl, just your sly glance from the far end of the table makes me think of a ship in Yemen, pulling into Mocha during 1760—the trade, the horses, the inventory. A pen-and-ink drawing of a man in a brocade floral gown holding a long thin brass pipe inlaid with mother of pearl, smoking.

Or while making love, the pleasure so visual, I am standing in a temple, simultaneously bending over to pick up a Venus figurine at my feet.

Like art, I am only attempting.

Like art, I don't know how to let love near.

Like art, your mouth leaning into mine is too much.

*Be still,* I want to say.

*Just be still.*

*Look.*

But that isn't the entire truth.

It would be most revealing to say: *I am afraid.*

But what I am most frightened to say is:

*Please. Sit here.*

*Read to me.*

# Notes and Acknowledgments

NOTES

"The Wilde Woman of Aiken"

> In 1882, Oscar Wilde toured the United States. Upon his arrival, many American critics, including comic-strip artists and photographers, chastised him for his theories on beauty. One photographer in particular, J. A. Palmer (Aiken, South Carolina), seeking to disprove Wilde's aesthetic—that anything could be beautiful—staged what he, Palmer, believed to be a satirical photo shoot, choosing objects he found to be inherently repugnant: highly patterned fabrics, an ornately upholstered chair, a sunflower, a face vessel, and a black woman.

"The Mothers"

> This poem is dedicated—with love and gratitude—to the sublime memory of Gwendolyn Brooks, and to the occupants of her "Kitchenette Building."

"Let Me Live in a House by the Side of the Road and
Be a Friend to Man"

> These poems are from an ongoing series in honor of the 1978 classic film *The Wiz*. Produced by Motown Productions and Universal Pictures, the film was a cinematic event. The first motion picture to be filmed at the historic Astoria Studios in New York, *The Wiz* was also the first U.S. film to include an entirely African-American cast. This series is dedicated to all those who participated in its production, most especially Lena Horne, Sidney Lumet, Geoffrey Holder,

Charlie Smalls, William F. Brown, Nipsey Russell, Ted Ross, Richard Pryor, Diana Ross, and Michael Jackson.

"Voyage of the Sable Venus"

"Voyage of the Sable Venus" is dedicated, with profound admiration, to the legacy of black librarianship, and black librarians, worldwide.

## ACKNOWLEDGMENTS

Grateful acknowledgment is made to the following publications, where a number of these poems first appeared:

American Academy of American Poets Poem-a-Day: "Summer"
*Callaloo:* "Red All Over" and "verga:"
*The Happy Hypocrite:* "Félicité"
*Lambda Literary Review:* "The Mothers"
*Los Angeles Review of Books:* "On the Road to Sri Bhuvaneshwari"
*Phantom Limb:* "The Body in August," "Mother Church No. 3," and "Plantation"
*Transition:* "Frame" and "The Wilde Woman of Aiken"
*Winning Writers:* "Beauty's Nest" and "From:   To:"

"Red All Over" subsequently appeared in *The Encyclopedia Project, Vol. 2, F–K,* edited by Tisa Bryant, Miranda Mellis, and Kate Schatz (Encyclomedia, 2010). "The Body in August" and "Frame" subsequently appeared in *Wide Awake: Poets of Los Angeles and Beyond, Pacific Coast Poetry Series,* edited by Suzanne Lummis (Beyond Baroque Books, 2015).

The following poems first appeared in these anthologies:

"Lure" originally appeared in *Cave Canem Anthology XII: 2008–2009,* edited by Randall Horton and Alison Meyers (Willow Books, 2012). Excerpts from "Voyage of the Sable Venus" originally appeared in *The Best of Kore Press 2012: Poetry,* edited by Ann Dernier (Kore Press, 2013).

"a dream of foxes"

in the dream of foxes
there is a field
and a procession of women
clean as good children
no hollow in the world
surrounded by dogs
no fur clumped bloody
on the ground
only a lovely line
of honest women stepping
without fear or guilt or shame
safe through the generous fields
—LUCILLE CLIFTON

*with gratitude:*

J. Bob Alotta, Dunya 'Alwan, Lee Azus, Rosebud Ben-Oni, Holly Blake, Janalynn Bliss, Pamela D. Bridgewater, Andrea Carter Brown, Vincent Brown, Sara Bruya, Tisa Bryant, Glenda Carpio, Ama Codjoe, the Coleman Family, Donna DeSouza, Kaila DeSouza, Denis Donoghue, Corinne Fitzpatrick, Jameson Fitzpatrick, Brian Francis, Jonterri Gadson, Chitra Ganesh, Helaine Gawlica, Hafizah Geter, Aracelis Girmay, Kimiko Hahn, Rob Halpern, Reginald Harris, Yona Harvey, Terrance Hayes, April Heck, Evelyn Brooks Higginbotham, Constance Vallis Hill, Page Hodel, Fanny Howe, Elisabeth Houston, Angela Jackson, Linda Susan Jackson, Madhu Kaza, Sara Kershnar, Mike Lala, Christine Larusso, Andrea Lawlor, Dorothy Lee, Helen Lee, Jordon Lee, Krishnakali Lewis, Vaishnavi Lewis, John Lucas, Ula Lucas, Kara Lynch, Kristin Maffei, Virginia McClure, JoAnne McFarland, Mary McHenry, Bernadine Mellis, Miranda Mellis, Julia Meltzer, Amina Meltzer-Thorne, Alison Meyers, Liz Miller, Jerome Murphy, Margaret Musgrove, Taura Musgrove, Alondra Nelson, Maggie Nelson, Marilyn Nelson, Mendi and Keith Obadike, Denise O'Malley, Greg Pardlo, Nina Payne, Geneva Perry, Kaye Perry, London Perry, Maya Popa, Carl Phillips, Toshi Reagon, Cat Richardson, Ed Robeson, Matthew Rohrer, Metta Sama, Kate Schatz, Nicole Sealey, Danzy Senna, Svati Shah, Charif Shanahan, Matthew Sharpe, Ellie Siegel, Michael Simonson, Tracy K. Smith, Adam Soldofsky, Anna Joy Springer, Louise Steinman, Zachary Sussman, Javid Syed, Nisa Tang, David Thorne, lê thi diem thúy,

Lynne Tillman, Jennifer Tseng, Steve Turner, Wendy S. Walters, Arisa White, Simone White, Dennis Williams, L. Lamar Wilson, Jenny Xie, Joanna Yas, Sarah Zapiler, and Rachel Zucker.

*for the immeasurable gifts of both time and confidence:*

The Headlands Center for the Arts, the Caldera Foundation, Summer Literary Seminars Kenya, the Ragdale Foundation. New York University's MFA writing community, especially Deborah Landau, Sharon Olds, and Yusef Komunyakaa, supported the writing of this book. Thank you, as well, to the USC PhD in Creative Writing & Literature Program, especially Percival Everett, Kate Flint, and David St. John; and to the USC Visual Studies Research Institute, especially Vanessa Schwartz and Akira Lippit. Most of all, to the inimitable Cave Canem Foundation, thank you: Toi Derricotte and Cornelius Eady.

*and for all the love and faith anyone could ever need:*

Elizabeth Alexander, Sheila Coleman, Alice Flaherty, Deborah Garrison, Judith Goldman, Adrienne Perry, Alice Quinn, Mala Rafik, Claudia Rankine, and Candice Watkins.

Finally, to my parents, Henry and Barbara Lewis, who committed the profoundly progressive act of taking a black girl's intellectual development seriously, I hope this book helps to repay the debt our society owes you and others like you. Thank you for convincing us—in spite of the world's lackluster narrative—that we were of interest and embodied a dynamic history.

Henri, you six-year-old wonder. Recently you said, "In the middle of Love Street and Heart Plaza, there's us." Thank you for choosing me.

Robin Coste Lewis, the winner of the National Book Award for *Voyage of the Sable Venus,* is the poet laureate of Los Angeles. She is writer-in-residence at the University of Southern California, as well as a Cave Canem fellow and a fellow of the Los Angeles Institute for the Humanities. She received her BA from Hampshire College, her MFA in poetry from New York University, an MTS in Sanskrit and comparative religious literature from the Divinity School at Harvard University, and a PhD in poetry and visual studies from the University of Southern California. Lewis was born in Compton, California; her family is from New Orleans.

A NOTE ON THE TYPE

This book was set in Adobe Garamond. Designed for the Adobe Corporation by Robert Slimbach, the fonts are based on types first cut by Claude Garamond (ca. 1480–1561). Garamond was a pupil of Geoffroy Tory and is believed to have followed the Venetian models, although he introduced a number of important differences, and it is to him that we owe the letter we now know as "old style." He gave to his letters a certain elegance and feeling of movement that won their creator an immediate reputation and the patronage of Francis I of France.

Composed by North Market Street Graphics,
Lancaster, Pennsylvania

Printed and bound by Berryville Graphics,
Berryville, Virginia